WIL

australia

Ken Stepnell

First published in 2015 by Reed New Holland Publishers Pty Ltd
London • Sydney • Auckland

The Chandlery, Unit 704, 50 Westminster Bridge Road, London SE1 7QY, UK
1/66 Gibbes Street, Chatswood, NSW 2067, Australia
5/39 Woodside Avenue, Northcote, Auckland 0627, New Zealand

www.newhollandpublishers.com

A record of this book is held at the British Library and the National Library
of Australia.

ISBN 978 1 92151 755 6

Managing Director: Fiona Schultz
Publisher and Project Editor: Simon Papps
Designer: Thomas Casey
Production Director: Olga Dementiev
Printer: Toppan Leefung Printing Ltd

10 9 8 7 6 5 4 3 2 1

Keep up with New Holland Publishers on Facebook
www.facebook.com/NewHollandPublishers

CONTENTS

Introduction 4

Flower families

BLANDFORDIACEAE Christmas bells 10

IRIDACEAE Irises 11

ORCHIDACEAE Orchids 12

XANTHORRHOEACEAE Day lilies and grass trees 57

HAEMODORACEAE Kangaroo paws 59

PROTEACEAE Banksias, dryandras, grevilleas, hakeas and allies . 64

DILLENIACEAE Guinea flowers 102

HALORAGACEAE Popflowers 104

AMARANTHACEAE Amaranths 105

DROSERACEAE Sundews..108

CUNONIACEAE Baueras 109

ELAEOCARPACEAE Pink-bells.......................................110

FABACEAE Peas and wattles 111

MYRTACEAE Myrtles, paperbarks, bottlebrushes and allies 129

MALVACEAE Mallows and hibiscuses.............................160

THYMELAEACEAE Pimeleas 162

RUTACEAE Citruses 164

ERICACEAE Heaths..166

LAMIACEAE Snake-bush and mint-bush 171

LENTIBULARIACEAE Fairy aprons..................................173

SCROPHULARIACEAE Turkey bush.................................174

SOLANACEAE Wild tomato 175

ASTERACEAE Daisies 176

GOODENIACEAE Dampieras, leschenaultias and allies.............180

STYLIDIACEAE Crab claws and trigger-plant 184

Glossary 186

Index...188

INTRODUCTION

Australian wild flowers

Australia's flora is very special. The famous botanist J.D. Hooker wrote that the country contains more unique plant species than any other place of a similar size. Upwards of about two-fifths of the genera and about seven-eights of the species in Australia are not found anywhere else around the world.

The flora in Australia is renowned for its richness and variety. The primitive appearance of many of the plants is strangely fascinating, as well as the areas in which they grow. Some favour small cracks in between rocks and live in complete solitude, while others make a carpet of colour in the vast inland region of Australia. Mountain areas can also become a blaze of colour when species such as Snow Daisy are in bloom.

Special adaptations

A great number of Australia's native flowers are xerophytes (drought-resistant) and these can be identified by their hardy leaves which are stiff, leathery and sharply pointed or divided. Many native flowers prevent water-loss through a covering of soft hairs, wax or cuticles, which protect them to some extent, without cutting off the air supply, hence the grey-green colour of much of our flora's foliage.

Introduction

In areas where the soil is open, the water remains for only a short time around the roots. Many of the plants have thick fleshy leaves and the plant stores water in these for later use. Some plants, including native orchids, can live and thrive for over a year without water.

The seeds of many plants will stay dormant for years in the soil until conditions are suitable for regeneration, usually after fire. These plants flower profusely for some years, then disappear only to resurface later when the cycle is repeated. Many species of native orchids and flowers appear only after fire, then all traces of them are lost until the next fire. So in certain cases fire is not always a bad thing for our plants.

Threats

Unfortunately many of our plants have disappeared over the years, either nationally or locally, often due to land-clearance for development or too many bush fires. Experts believe that over 70 species of plants have been lost since Australia was settled and over 200 species of plants are on the endangered list.

No doubt each day the threat becomes worse. Settlement and progress cannot be blamed entirely for the loss of species. Alien species, introduced both by accident and on purpose, have become a threat to native flowers in many areas. Hopefully increasing public awareness and pride will help to control the spread of these plants that are now called weeds. The Field Naturalist Groups and the Society for Growing Native Plants are just two of the organisations that have encouraged home gardeners to plant their own native gardens.

To some travellers, just seeing a variety of native flowers on a roadside verge has been enough to convert them into being a flower lover. Unfortunately, in many areas these are now the only places where native flowers can be found in any great numbers; progress has overtaken species that were growing on farms or in bush land. Crown lands or national parks will contain many species of native flowers, and perhaps these areas may be the 'saviour' for some of our plants.

Wild flower highlights

In the eyes of many people Western Australia is the jewel in the crown in terms of native flora, and to botanists it is known as 'the wildflower state'. After some of the early explorers thought it was an uninspiring place, the likes of Von Muller and his botanists proved that it was unique in terms of the variety of plants that could be found. This is still the case today.

More and more people are becoming interested in plants, both for relaxation and enjoyment. It is hoped that this may slow the rate of destruction of many of the world's endangered plants and habitats. Tourism is also helping to make people from all walks of life aware of our native flowers, and this has helped with many varieties of native plants now being grown in nurseries around Australia.

I hope that this guide will help the dedicated nature enthusiast and the next generation of flower lovers to appreciate the enormous variety of special plants that are found in our country. The words and descriptions will hopefully be of use to everyone, including beginners. Hopefully it will contribute towards more people appreciating nature in all its glory.

The species in this book.

As much as possible this guide attempts to cover common and widespread species, and it also includes some of the specialities from particular regions, states, territories or habitats.

The flowers are listed in taxonomic order by family. The order broadly follows the APG (Angiosperm Phylogeny Group) III system of flowering plant classification, which is a modern, mostly molecular-based, system.

The Latin name is listed alongside the common name. It is a must for all people who are interested in flora to use these botanical names. Common names are not always universally applied and there are still some local and regional variations.

Each species account gives at least one photograph for identification and also a concise description of the plant's form, its leaves, flowers and other key identification features. The 'Habitat/ Range' section is also of particular importance for ID, as a flower which is a speciality of one particular soil-type or region is unlikely to occur elsewhere.

THE FLOWERS

Christmas Bells *Blandfordia nobilis*

HEIGHT/ID: 80cm. An upright perennial plant, with a few leaves at the base of the stem – these are like grass and can be up to 80cm long.

FLOWERS: Red flowers are tipped with six yellow lobes. They are bell-shaped, up to 4cm long and 1cm wide. Usually arranged in sets of 3–10 flowers. Flowers from winter to spring.

HABITAT/RANGE: Prefers wet heathland and swampland of coastal New South Wales.

Purple Flags *Patersonia occidentalis*

HEIGHT/ID: 55cm. A small tufted perennial herb. Long, smooth and hairless leaves are shaped like a sword and grow to 55cm.

FLOWERS: Up to 7cm across. Blue or violet, they have three large and very conspicuous petals. Flowers in spring.

HABITAT/RANGE: Grows in most of the temperate areas of New South Wales, Victoria, Tasmania, South Australia and Western Australia.

Giant Boat-lip Orchid *Cymbidium madidum*

HEIGHT/ID: 40cm. Has long strap-like leaves and large seed-pods.

FLOWERS: The pendulous spray of these flowers, along with the fragrant perfume, are a characteristic part of the tropics. Flowers can be green to yellow, are about 3cm across and last about two weeks. Flowers from winter to spring.

HABITAT/RANGE: Grows on rotting logs and forks in trees in areas of tropical Queensland and New South Wales. Often found in rainforests.

Grassy Boat-lip Orchid *Cymbidium suave*

HEIGHT/ID: 70cm. One of the orchid species that grows into clumps. Stems are narrow, but are able to extend for some distance while growing.

FLOWERS: Colour varies from dark green to green or brownish, often they are blotched. Grow to 3cm across. The racemes are arched almost to the point of being pendulous. Flowers winter to spring.

HABITAT/RANGE: Hollow tree limbs, old tree stumps and rotting timber are favourite places for these orchids. Coastal areas of rainforest and tropical regions of Queensland and New South Wales.

Red Beaks Orchid *Pyrorchis nigricans*

HEIGHT/ID: 50cm. The fleshy leaf is rotund to ovate and is from 2–6cm wide.

FLOWERS: Each stout stem is usually from 2–6cm. Blooms are dark reddish in colour. The hood-like dorsal sepal is prominently striped with red or purple. Has spreading lateral sepals and the petals are linear. Flowers in spring.

HABITAT/RANGE: Grows in a variety of soils and conditions in Western Australia, South Australia, New South Wales, Victoria and Tasmania. Flowers well after fire.

Grampians Leafy Greenhood *Bunochilus macilentus*

HEIGHT/ID: 30cm. Stem is erect with sword-shaped leaves to 4cm long. The stem clasps the flowers and the leaves are arranged in a rosette.

FLOWERS: As many as 10 blooms can occur on the stem. Flowers are light green, the dorsal tips have pale orange markings, and they occur in loose racemes. Flowers in spring.

HABITAT/RANGE: Moist and well-drained areas suit this species, which is found over much of Victoria.

Blunt Greenhood *Pterostylis curta*

HEIGHT/ID: 30cm. Perennial and erect. Leaves are flat, oval and tapered at each end. One flower per stem, stems can be 25cm tall.

FLOWERS: White with green stripes and often soft green all over. The middle sepal forms the hood, the other two sepals are slightly curled with the tip pointed. The lateral sepal is slightly pointed upwards, rarely above the hood. Flowers in spring.

HABITAT/RANGE: Coasts and any moist areas of Victoria, New South Wales, Tasmania and South Australia.

Alpine Greenhood *Pterostylis alpina*

HEIGHT/ID: 40cm. Perennial and erect. Leaves are oval, flat and tapered at the end; they can be up to 4cm long.

FLOWERS: Pale green flowers, usually to 3cm long. The labellum tip protrudes a short distance through the flower. The dorsal sepal is blunt-tipped and the sepal points curve backwards. Flowers in spring.

HABITAT/RANGE: Not strictly alpine and occurs at different altitudes throughout the high country of New South Wales, Victoria and Tasmania.

Nodding Greenhood *Pterostylis nutans*

HEIGHT/ID: 30cm. Perennial and erect. Leaves are flat, oval and pointed at the end.

FLOWERS: White with some green stripes, can often be green with white on the bonnet. The hood on the bonnet is formed by the middle sepal, other sepals are bent towards the tip and sometimes curved. Flowers in spring.

HABITAT/RANGE: Found in heathland, open forest country, both wet and dry forests and coastal areas of Victoria, New South Wales, South Australia, Tasmania and Queensland.

Blotched Cane Orchid *Thelychiton gracilicaulis*

HEIGHT/ID: 10cm. Thin, notched leaves which are yellow to greenish.

FLOWERS: From 5–10 flowers about 1.3cm across. Flowers often droop. They are often yellow with large reddish or brown spots on the outside. Sepals and petals spread and slightly incurved, they are thick and partly fleshy. Flowers winter to spring.

HABITAT/RANGE: Rainforest, moist areas and humid areas of Queensland and New South Wales.

Scarlet Greenhood *Diplodium coccinum*

HEIGHT/ID: 30cm. Leaves are arranged in a rosette and are sword-shaped. They are large and often bluish-green. Labellum long and protruding.

FLOWERS: Deep maroon to reddish flower, but can also be green with a brown tip. Usually the flower leans forward, with only one flower per stem. Flowers in summer.

HABITAT/RANGE: Grasslands and open forest areas of New South Wales, Victoria, Queensland and Tasmania.

Swamp Greenhood *Diplodium tenuissimum*

HEIGHT/ID: 30cm. A slender stem and a few small, thin, dark green leaves. Labellum is lance-pointed and curved.

FLOWERS: Small and slender on the stem, not quite 1cm wide. Nearly white with green markings. They are slightly curved, the dorsal sepal has a long thread-like apex. Flowers spring to summer.

HABITAT/RANGE: Prefers swamp areas, in particular under Woolly Tea Tree, in areas of Victoria and South Australia.

Jug Orchid *Stamnorchis recurva*

HEIGHT/ID: 45cm. A leafy stemmed plant, unusual because it has the horned lateral sepals more prominent than the hood.

FLOWERS: Large and jug-shaped flowers, which can be several centimetres long. They are greenish with white stripes and red to brown points. The labellum is enclosed in the flower. Flowers in spring.

HABITAT/RANGE: Found from Geraldton to Israelite Bay in Western Australia.

Boorman's Rustyhood *Oligochaetochilus boormanii*

HEIGHT/ID: 20cm. Leaves set in a rosette.

FLOWERS: May have up to eight blooms – each 1.3cm in diameter – these hang forward as though they are nodding. The labellum is thick and broad, while the lateral sepals are turned down and flare from the base. Dorsal petal long and pointed with incurved edges. Flowers are reddish-brown on a green stem. Flowers in spring.

HABITAT/RANGE: Found in a variety of regions, especially favours rocky areas of Queensland, New South Wales, Victoria and South Australia.

Bearded Greenhood *Plumatichilos plumosum*

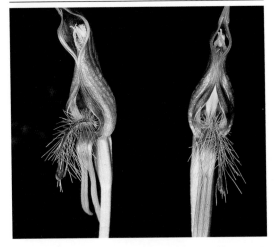

HEIGHT/ID: 25cm. From 5–20 ground-hugging, fleshy and lance-shaped leaves.

FLOWERS: Very translucent green with dark green net marking usually shiny. The dorsal sepal point can be to 1–2cm long and is nearly always curved. Pale yellow thread-like labellum hangs out about 2cm and is covered with tiny hairs. Flowers winter to spring.

HABITAT/RANGE: Grows in open forest areas and some grasslands in New South Wales, Victoria, Tasmania and South Australia.

Slender Sun Orchid *Thelymitra pauciflora*

HEIGHT/ID: 40cm. Perennial. Stem erect. Has solitary leaf which is narrow, linear and partially channelled.

FLOWERS: From 1–5 blue flowers on the stem. Each is 2cm across and they sheath at the base of the stem. Flowers in spring.

HABITAT/RANGE: Open heathland and forest regions of Queensland, New South Wales, Australian Capital Territory, Victoria, South Australia and Tasmania.

Spotted Sun Orchid *Thelymitra ixioides*

HEIGHT/ID: 60cm. Erect perennial. Leaves narrow and up to 20cm long.

FLOWERS: Usually blue, but occasionally pink or purple. Flowers are about 3cm across and often spotted black on upper petals. Several flowers per stalk. Flowers winter to spring.

HABITAT/RANGE: In forests, woodlands and coastal ranges of Western Australia, Queensland, New South Wales, Victoria and Tasmania.

Salmon Sun Orchid *Thelymitra rubra*

HEIGHT/ID: 42cm. Leaves are linear and about 11cm long. Bracts very narrow.

FLOWERS: About 2cm across, either one or two flowers per stem. Six petals, colour from salmon pink to pale pink. Petals and sepals egg-shaped. Flowers in spring.

HABITAT/RANGE: Coastal areas, heathlands and open forest areas of New South Wales, Victoria, Tasmania and South Australia.

Queen of Sheba *Thelymitra speciosa*

HEIGHT/ID: 30cm. Leaf can be twisted or spiral-shaped; base usually purple and can be blotched.

FLOWERS: From 1–5 flowers per stem. Colour is iridescent orange, purple, red or pink or variegated with a variety of shades, blotches or some streaks.

HABITAT/RANGE: Grows among low shrubs on heathlands of southern Western Australia. Widespread but rarely seen. Requires warm microclimate.

Great Sun Orchid *Thelymitra aristata*

HEIGHT/ID: 80cm. Has a single leaf, which is leathery, linear and pointed; it is often bluish-green and can be spotted. Terrestrial and only apparent above ground-level during the spring or summer growth period.

FLOWERS: Flowering stems can have up to 40 blooms. Flowers deep blue, sometimes lilac, each up to 6cm in diameter, sometimes many blooms are open at once. Flowers in spring.

HABITAT/RANGE: Open forest country, woodlands and swamp areas of New South Wales, Victoria and Tasmania, including both King and Flinders Islands.

Daddy Long-legs Orchid *Caladenia filamentosa*

HEIGHT/ID: 45cm. Leaf is narrow, but erect and spreading and the tips droop.

FLOWERS: Flower segments are long and thin, yellowish, white or reddish. Sepals and petals are covered with fine glands, but none at the base of the column. Flowers in spring.

HABITAT/RANGE: Grows in a variety of different soil types. Areas of Queensland, New South Wales, Australian Capital Territory, Victoria, Tasmania and South Australia.

Pink Fairy Orchid *Caladenia latifolia*

HEIGHT/ID: 50cm. Small perennial. Leaf is small, lancelote, usually prostrate and grows to 18cm long. Underside of leaf is soft reddish. Stem is very erect and grows to about 40cm.

FLOWERS: Dark pink flowers up to 3cm wide. Flowers winter to spring.

HABITAT/RANGE: In open forest country and heathland of New South Wales, Australian Capital Territory, Victoria, Tasmania and Flinders Island. Subspecies from Western Australia is illustrated.

Clubbed Spider Orchid *Caladenia clavigera*

HEIGHT/ID: 20cm. Perennial. Stem erect and slender, with a solitary leaf which can be up to 18cm long and sword-shaped; the undersurface is spotted.

FLOWERS: Red and green flower usually about 5cm across, sepals are reddish with black ends. Labellum heart-shaped, green to whitish, and tips usually rounded. Flowers in spring.

HABITAT/RANGE: Found in a variety of habitats, but especially favours open forest areas of New South Wales, Australian Capital Territory, South Australia, Victoria, Tasmania and Flinders Island.

Large Spider Orchid *Caladenia longicauda*

HEIGHT/ID: 60cm. Usually in clumps of a few plants, but can also be solitary. Leaf up to 20cm long and 2cm wide and slightly hairy on upper surface. Lateral sepals can be 12mm wide.

FLOWERS: Spectacular white flowers grow to several centimetres across, the petals have long thread-like pieces hanging down. Labellum heart-shaped. Flowers in spring.

HABITAT/RANGE: Widespread over much of Western Australia, from Geraldton to Esperance, in open forest, bushland and heathland areas.

Dwarf Jester Orchid
Caladenia bryceana ssp. *bryceana*

HEIGHT/ID: 3cm. Leaf grows to about 1.2cm and can have reddish colour. Sepals and petals are short as well.

FLOWERS: Grow to around 2cm and may also have reddish tinge on petals. Labellum has a downward curve, which is green with a red apex. Flowers in spring.

HABITAT/RANGE: Very restricted distribution in the Stirling Ranges of Western Australia.

Tongue Orchid *Cryptostylis subulata*

HEIGHT/ID: 80cm. Leaves lanceolate, dark green to yellow on both sides. Leaves absent at flowering time.

FLOWERS: Green to yellowish flowers 5cm across, they occur in erect terminal racemes with several blooms. Both sepals and petals are yellowish. Flowers winter to autumn.

HABITAT/RANGE: Often found among rushes in swamp areas and damp regions of Victoria, Queensland, New South Wales, Tasmania and South Australia.

Flying Duck Orchid *Caleana major*

HEIGHT/ID: 35cm. Small and erect. Leaves narrow, sword-like and grow to 10cm.

FLOWERS: Dark reddish to brown, some may have green sepals and petals. Resembles a duck in flight – labellum is attached by a small claw and forms duck's head. Flowers winter to spring.

HABITAT/RANGE: Open heathlands, open forests and woodlands of Victoria, New South Wales, Queensland, Tasmania and South Australia.

Hyacinth Orchid *Dipodium punctatum*

HEIGHT/ID: 1m. Leafless herb with a dark and robust stem.

FLOWERS: Pale pink to a deep pink, often with dark spots. Flower up to 2cm across, spoon-shaped lip can have a white beard. Up to 40 or 50 flower-heads on one stalk. Petals and sepals are all free and spreading. Flowers in spring.

HABITAT/RANGE: Widespread in forests, dry open woodlands and coastal ranges in Victoria, Queensland and New South Wales.

King Orchid *Dendrobium speciosum*

HEIGHT/ID: Grows on host tree. Leaves up to 30cm long.

FLOWERS: Perfumed creamy-white to yellow flowers can be 3cm across. Limbs up to 70cm long, each has many flowers – up to 100 is not uncommon. Petals oblong and pointed. One of the best-known tropical orchids. Flowers winter to spring.

HABITAT/RANGE: Widespread in coastal areas and rocky habitats in Queensland, New South Wales and parts of eastern Victoria.

Pink Fingers *Petalochilus carneus*

HEIGHT/ID: 25cm. Stem erect and slender with a single leaf, which is broad, hairy and about 20cm long, as well as having a musky odour.

FLOWERS: White or pink, some may have a dark band on lower petal. Up to four blooms on the one stem. Dorsal sepal erect and the red-barred lip on flower is conspicuous. Flowers in spring.

HABITAT/RANGE: Open forest areas and grasslands of Queensland, New South Wales, Australian Capital Territory, Victoria, Tasmania and South Australia.

Purple Enamel Orchid *Elythranthera brunonis*

HEIGHT/ID: 15cm. Perennial with erect stem and very hairy solitary leaf with a spread of about 10cm.

FLOWERS: Rich purple and glossy, these are very striking in a bush setting. Flowers up to 3cm across, petal almost 1cm and usually curved, 1–2 flowers per stem. Flowers winter to summer.

HABITAT/RANGE: Grows in a variety of soils in south-west Western Australia.

Pink Enamel Orchid *Elythranthera emarginata*

HEIGHT/ID: 30cm. Solitary, hairy, oval-shaped leaf with a dark reddish-green base. Stem erect.

FLOWERS: Brilliant pink and glossy, they occur in clusters of up to three blooms 5cm across. Flowers can be blotched with dark red or purple. Flowers winter to spring.

HABITAT/RANGE: Grows in a variety of soils and conditions in southern Western Australia.

Scented Leek Orchid *Prasophyllum odoratum*

HEIGHT/ID: 80cm. Perennial. Solitary cylindrical leaf is present when plant in flower.

FLOWERS: Flowers up to 1cm across and well spaced with up to 10 per stem. Flowers greenish-brown with white or pink petals, the prominent labellum is white or brown. Flowers in spring.

HABITAT/RANGE: Grows well in poor, well-drained soils of South Australia and Victoria.

Dainty Blue China Orchid *Cyanicula amplexans*

HEIGHT/ID: 25cm. Leaf often prostrate and in most cases broad.

FLOWERS: Pale blue labellum with a white or light cream calli. Flowers triple-lobed, the centre lobe incurved and slightly shorter than the others. Flowers winter to spring.

HABITAT/RANGE: Occurs in open areas of scrub and woodland in south-west Western Australia.

Common Golden Moths *Diuris chryseopsis*

HEIGHT/ID: 30cm. Leaves are straight, as is the flower stem.

FLOWERS: Flowers yellow and can have some dark internal streaks. Up to four flower-heads can be found on each stem. The petals are almost horizontal to partly drooping. Flowers in spring.

HABITAT/RANGE: Favours moist soils. Found in open grassland areas, forest regions and swamplands in New South Wales, Victoria, Tasmania and South Australia.

Western Purple Donkey Orchid *Diuris daltonii*

HEIGHT/ID: 40cm. Two leaves which are about 0.5cm wide and folded.

FLOWERS: Dark purple flower-heads are about 3cm in diameter. Petals usually erect.

HABITAT/RANGE: Open forest and red gum areas of Victoria and South Australia.

Green Bird Orchid *Simpliglottis cornuta*

HEIGHT/ID: 5cm. Leaves usually about 0.3cm wide.

FLOWERS: Colour of flowers varies from green to reddish-green and the petals are incurved slightly. The labellum is erect and heart-shaped, and the tip is often reddish to brown. Flowers spring to summer.

HABITAT/RANGE: Widespread and still common in moist open forest areas of New South Wales, Victoria and Tasmania.

Common Elbow Orchid *Thynninorchis huntianus*

HEIGHT/ID: 15cm. Stem is very wiry and thin, colour varies from green to red.

FLOWERS: The flower-heads look like tiny insects and are greenish to reddish in colour.

HABITAT/RANGE: Grows in most types of soil in areas of New South Wales, Australian Capital Territory, Victoria, Tasmania and Flinders Island.

Small Helmet Orchid *Anzybas unguiculatus*

HEIGHT/ID: 3cm. Perennial. Stem short and erect. Flat and oval solitary leaf is green with a red-grey under-surface.

FLOWERS: Maroon flower about 1cm in diameter and hooded. One flower per stalk. Flowers autumn to spring.

HABITAT/RANGE: In a variety of areas of New South Wales, Victoria, Tasmania and South Australia.

Stately Helmet Orchid *Corysanthes diemenica*

HEIGHT/ID: 4cm. In some cases the leaf is almost as large as the flower, barely 2cm. The leaf is bright green on the top and underneath a silvery green.

FLOWERS: Flower has an almost bird-like profile, it is about 1.5cm in diameter. Petals can be erect or recurved – they are dark red with transparent mottles. Flowers winter to summer.

HABITAT/RANGE: Grows in a variety of soils, but often found in rotted leaf-mould areas of the bushland in Queensland, New South Wales, Victoria and Tasmania.

Purple Beard Orchid *Calochilus robertsonii*

HEIGHT/ID: 40cm. Leaves fully developed when the plant flowers — they are about 1.2cm, and not much larger than the flower.

FLOWERS: Petals brown to greenish in colour with fine purple stripes. Mauve or white labellum has hair-like structures that resemble a beard. Flower usually only lasts a few days. Flowers winter to spring.

HABITAT/RANGE: Found in parts of Victoria, Queensland, South Australia, Tasmania and Australian Capital Territory.

Rattle Beaks *Lyperanthus serratus*

HEIGHT/ID: 40cm. Erect stem appears a little stout. Solitary leaf is sword-shaped, pointed and grows to around 30cm.

FLOWERS: Green flowers tinged with yellow, brown or reddish. Can be 2cm in diameter with long narrow petals and a curved dorsal sepal. Up to eight blooms per stem. Flowers in spring.

HABITAT/RANGE: Grows in a variety of conditions in southern Western Australia and occurs mainly in the Gin Gin district.

Banded Bee Orchid *Diuris laxiflora*

HEIGHT/ID: 8cm. A slender member of its genus with narrow and straight leaves.

FLOWERS: Yellow with dark blotches scattered over the flowers. Petals are erect and can be recurved. Flowers can be 2cm across. Flowers winter to spring.

HABITAT/RANGE: Found in grassland areas and some open forest country of Western Australia.

Common Potato Orchid *Gastrodia sesamoides*

HEIGHT/ID: 20cm. Flower stem is tall, slender, brown, fleshy and smooth.

FLOWERS: Tubular in appearance, usually light brown to whitish and with a slight fragrance. The flowers are bell-shaped and hang in loose racemes, which are usually 2cm long. Stem can have upwards of 25 flowers. Flowers in summer.

HABITAT/RANGE: Prefers damper areas of wet forests and mountain ranges of New South Wales, Victoria, Australian Capital Territory and Tasmania.

Erect Pencil Orchid *Dockrillia racemosa*

HEIGHT/ID: 120cm. Named because of its long cylindrical leaves. The long branched stems are initially erect and become pendulous as they grow.

FLOWERS: The slender white or yellowish-white flowers are about 2.5cm across. The flowers are not crowded on the stem like many other native orchids. Flowers in spring.

HABITAT/RANGE: Always associated with mountain or rainforest areas where conditions are cool and moist.

Streaked Rock Orchid *Dockrillia striolata*

HEIGHT/ID: 20cm. Leaves erect and pendulous and can be curved and often slender in appearance. The plant has a few small branches and the roots are open.

FLOWERS: Colour varies from creamy-yellow to greenish-brown. Up to 12 flowers per stalk. Flowers in spring.

HABITAT/RANGE: Occurs on rocks and sandstone cliffs in parts of New South Wales, Victoria and Tasmania, as well as on both Flinders and Cape Barren Islands.

Fragrant Tea-tree Orchid *Cepobaculum semifuscum*

HEIGHT/ID: 40cm. Leaves on the upper node are usually dark green. Racemes are up to 40cm long.

FLOWERS: Up to 20 yellow to brownish flower-heads with twisted shiny dorsal petals. Labellum narrow and slightly scented. Flowers about 3cm in diameter. Flowers winter to spring.

HABITAT/RANGE: Grows in forest and woodland on the trunks of melaleuca trees. Occurs in humid areas of north Queensland.

Banded Tree Spider Orchid
Tetrabaculum tetragonum

HEIGHT/ID: Grows on host tree and usually hangs downwards. Has a number of leaves, which typically are dark green.

FLOWERS: Greenish to yellow with narrow dark brown bands. Dorsal sepal very erect and can be 10cm long. Flowers winter to spring.

HABITAT/RANGE: Most commonly found growing on trees or rocks, and often near water. Occurs in coastal and mountain areas of New South Wales and Queensland.

Bonnet Orchid *Cryptostylis erecta*

HEIGHT/ID: 12cm. Leaves sword-shaped can be up to 3cm across.

FLOWERS: Flower stems can be 10cm and have up to 12 flowers per stem. Greenish to lilac flower about 1.5cm in diameter. Labellum egg-shaped with pointed tip and dark red markings and forms part of bonnet or hood on flower. Flowers winter to autumn.

HABITAT/RANGE: Found in a variety of soil-types in Queensland, New South Wales and Victoria.

Pink Spiral Orchid *Spiranthes australis*

HEIGHT/ID: 45cm. Dark green shiny leaves about 1cm across – they are erect, partly sword-shaped, and form a rosette.

FLOWERS: Stem can be 45cm high and have more than 50 flower-heads arranged in a spiral. Flower usually bright pink with a white labellum. Dorsal sepal and petals overlap to form a tube. Flowers in summer.

HABITAT/RANGE: Most types of soils in open country, marsh, swamps and high rainfall areas of Queensland, Australian Capital Territory, New South Wales, Victoria, South Australia and Tasmania.

Fairy Bells *Sarcochilus ceciliae*

HEIGHT/ID: Lives on host tree. Leaves heavily pigmented and very fleshy. Thick root seeks out any crevices for moisture.

FLOWERS: Light pink or magenta flowers usually 1cm in diameter. Up to 30 flowers can be in bloom at once. Flowers in spring.

HABITAT/RANGE: Rocky areas and mountain ranges of Queensland and New South Wales. This is one of 14 *Sarcochilus* species in Australia and they only bloom in high rainfall areas on the east coast.

Large Boulder Orchid *Sarcochilus hartmannii*

HEIGHT/ID: 20cm. Grows in clumps. Plant is branched and has numerous thickly textured leaves on each stem.

FLOWERS: Numerous flowers crowd each stem. They are usually white with crimson and yellow centres, but can occasionally be all white. Flowers in spring.

HABITAT/RANGE: Grows on rocks and cliff faces in areas of Queensland, and New South Wales. Favours cool areas but needs some sun.

Green Antelope Orchid *Ceratobium dalbertisii*

HEIGHT/ID: Lives on host plant. Usually has green to yellow leaf. Stem is erect, can be dark green and is partly notched.

FLOWERS: A white flower with green petals, often curved to one side. Labellum mainly white with pale purple stripes. Flowers are long lasting. In flower from March until December.

HABITAT/RANGE: Very local in occurrence and found on high branches of rainforest trees in Queensland.

Wax-lip Orchid *Glossodia major*

HEIGHT/ID: 15cm. Deciduous. Has a very slender erect stem with a single dark green leaf at ground-level.

FLOWERS: Five-petalled flower usually purple, but also occasionally mauve and rarely white. Labellum white and mauve. Dorsal sepal mostly erect, but can sometimes be curved. Flowers late winter to spring.

HABITAT/RANGE: Grows in a variety of soils and conditions in Queensland, New South Wales, Australian Capital Territory, Victoria, South Australia and Tasmania.

Cooktown Orchid *Vappodes phalaenopsis*

HEIGHT/ID: 45cm. This epiphytic plant is native to north Queensland. The leaves are mainly ovate, ribbed and green.

FLOWERS: A very distinctive orchid. Flower colour is most frequently pink, but can sometimes be lilac or white. Some flowers have a white spot on the lip. Long branches contain many flowers, each about 4cm in diameter. Flowers from summer to autumn. The floral emblem of Queensland.

HABITAT/RANGE: From coastal areas to mountain ranges in Queensland.

Blotched Sun Orchid *Thelymitra benthamiana*

HEIGHT/ID: 40cm. Broad leaf is light green to yellow.

FLOWERS: Several yellow to greenish-yellow flowers with many dark or reddish spots on the petals. Flower up to 4cm in diameter. Flowers in spring.

HABITAT/RANGE: Grows in a variety of soils from open forest areas to heathlands of Western Australia, South Australia, Victoria, Tasmania and Flinders Island.

Leafless Parson's Bands *Eriochilus cucullatus*

HEIGHT/ID: 15cm. A ground-hugging plant. Grows from a single grey-green leaf which is usually ovate and can be up to 2cm long.

FLOWERS: From 1–3 delicately perfumed flowers on the same stem. The species is distinguishable by the two deflexed lateral sepals, which are usually longer and can be white or pale yellow. Flowers from summer to autumn.

HABITAT/RANGE: Occurs in open forest and grasslands of Queensland, New South Wales, Australian Capital Territory, Victoria, Tasmania and South Australia.

Nodding Blue Lily *Stypandra glauca*

HEIGHT/ID: 1m. Erect perennial herb. Stem-clasping leaves up to 15cm long and 1cm wide and arranged in opposite rows along the stem.

FLOWERS: Blue with six nodding stamens, yellow filaments hang loosely in branching clumps at the ends. Flower diameter 2cm. Flowers from spring to summer.

HABITAT/RANGE: Widespread in a variety of soils and conditions in Queensland, New South Wales, Victoria, South Australia and Western Australia.

Blue Tinsel-lily *Calectasia cyanea*

HEIGHT/ID: 1.5m. Very upright perennial with wiry stem. Leaves narrow and pointed, 3–5mm long and 1mm wide.

FLOWERS: Blue or deep purple flower is a five-pointed star, 10cm in diameter, with six protruding yellow stamens. Flowers from winter to spring.

HABITAT/RANGE: Prefers the well-drained sandy and forest areas of Victoria, South Australia and Western Australia.

Black Gin *Kingia australis*

HEIGHT/ID: 2m. Erect perennial with broad solitary trunk. Grey-green grass-like leaves to 60cm long; very hairy when plant young.

FLOWERS: Globular flower-heads cream to grey and grow from a stout stalk up to 50cm long. Flowers from winter to spring.

HABITAT/RANGE: Favours open heathlands in Western Australia.

Red-and-green Kangaroo Paw
Anigozanthos manglesii

HEIGHT/ID: 1m. Leaves rise from sheath at base of the plant. Each is about 50cm long and 1cm wide.

FLOWERS: Green and red tubular flowers up to 10cm long. Usually has six curled black lobes on one side of the flower, the other side is covered with thick green hairs. Flowers from winter to spring. The floral emblem of Western Australia.

HABITAT/RANGE: Found in sandy bush and forest areas of Western Australia, and also in a small area of south-eastern Queensland.

Green Kangaroo Paw *Anigozanthos viridis*

HEIGHT/ID: 50cm. A perennial herb. Plant dies down in summer. Slender leaves can grow to 50cm long.

FLOWERS: Tubular flowers green or yellow-green, slightly split on lower side with reflexed lobes to 7cm long. Blooms from winter to spring.

HABITAT/RANGE: Open heathlands and forest regions of Western Australia.

Common Cat's Paw *Anigozanthos humilis*

HEIGHT/ID: 20cm. Small perennial herb. Leaves up to 20cm long; flat and sickle-shaped, usually die down when finished flowering.

FLOWERS: Tubular flowers up to 5cm long. Mainly yellow, suffused with red or pink. Single flowering stem is hairy. Flowers from spring to summer.

HABITAT/RANGE: Prefers sandy soils and open woodlands in south-west Western Australia.

Red Kangaroo Paw *Anigozanthos rufus*

HEIGHT/ID: 40cm. Perennial. Grows in a clump. Strap-like leaves grow to 40cm and often rather dull grey-green.

FLOWERS: Tubular flowers up to 4cm long. Usually brilliant red, sometimes purple. Flowering stems woolly and can be several centimetres high. Flowers from spring to summer.

HABITAT/RANGE: Occurs in low heath areas and open country in south-west Western Australia.

Black Kangaroo Paw *Macropidia fuliginosa*

HEIGHT/ID: 1.5m. Strap-like leaves rise from base of plant in sheath-like manner, they grow to 30cm long and 10cm wide.

FLOWERS: Striking in appearance – mainly black with a green tubular stem and up to 6cm long. They have six curled lobes on one side of the flower and are covered with tiny black hairs. Flowers from late winter to spring.

HABITAT/RANGE: Prefers the stony, gravelly, heath and mallee areas of south-west Western Australia.

Albany Synaphea *Synaphea polymorpha*

HEIGHT/ID: 50cm. A small shrub with a reddish stem, oblong in appearance and with undivided basal leaves to 20cm long. Upper leaves are much shorter with stiff points.

FLOWERS: Yellow flowers and have lobed petals. Individual flowers are about 1cm long. Flowers from spring to summer.

HABITAT/RANGE: Open woodland and bushland regions of eastern Western Australia.

Mountain Devil *Lambertia formosa*

HEIGHT/ID: 2m. A tall bush-like shrub. Leaves wedge-shaped and pointed, up to 2cm long, shiny green on upperside and off-white underneath.

FLOWERS: Red and tubular, 4cm long with a bearded interior. These are arranged in a small terminal cluster of seven flowers which is enclosed in a red bract. Flowers at almost any time of year.

HABITAT/RANGE: Prefers sandy dry soil of the forest and heathland of New South Wales.

Narrow-leaved Drumsticks *Isopogon anethifolius*

HEIGHT/ID: 2m. Usually an erect shrub, but in some areas can be almost prostrate. Leaves up to 10cm long, flat, stiff and divided into at least three linear-pointed or spear-pointed shapes.

FLOWERS: Stalkless yellow flowers occur in dense terminal globules. The rounded flower-heads are about 4cm across. Flowers from early spring to summer.

HABITAT/RANGE: Occurs in areas of New South Wales and Queensland.

Isopogon sp. *Isopogon latifolius*

HEIGHT/ID: 2m. Evergreen shrub, erect and usually stout in appearance. Leaves grow to 10cm long by 4cm wide; they are thick, broad, flat and slightly pointed.

FLOWERS: Purple or magenta flowers appear in terminal heads in a mass of tubular flower-heads. They are curved upwards to about 4cm and have small tufts of hair at the ends of the apex.

HABITAT/RANGE: Well-drained soils in south-west Western Australia.

Monga Waratah *Telopea mongaensis*

HEIGHT/ID: 2m. Open and upright shrub. Leathery leaves are linear, slightly curved and can be up to 15cm long.

FLOWERS: Red flowers about 10cm across in a terminal cluster – when in full bloom flowers appear to be flattened. Flowers in spring.

HABITAT/RANGE: In bushland and sheltered forest in New South Wales and Victoria.

Waratah *Telopea speciosissima*

HEIGHT/ID: 4m. Tall erect shrub. Leaves feel leathery and are narrow and oblong with serrated margins; they grow up to 25cm long and 4cm wide.

FLOWERS: Brilliant crimson-red tubular flowers with four curled lobes at the back and a white-tipped style at the terminal head. Flower-heads up to 15cm across. Flowers in spring.

HABITAT/RANGE: Coastal regions, mainly in the sandy soils of New South Wales and isolated areas of Victoria.

Prostrate Banksia *Banksia gardneri*

HEIGHT/ID: Prostrate shrub with strong, spreading, hairy branches. Linear leaves tend to be erect and stiff and appear from the base of the cone. Fully-grown sword-shaped leaves can be 40cm long and 8cm wide.

FLOWERS: Tubular flowers vary in colour from brown to soft yellow. Erect flower cone can be 10cm long and grows almost from ground-level. Flowers from spring into summer.

HABITAT/RANGE: Sandy heathlands of south-west Western Australia.

Silver Banksia *Banksia marginata*

HEIGHT/ID: Up to 10m; size depends on location. Can be a tall shrub, but often is only a small bush. Rough pale grey bark. Leaves narrow and obovate, dark green on top and off-white underneath, up to 5cm long and evenly spiked.

FLOWERS: Spikes can be 10cm long and 6cm across, usually pale yellow, styles also yellow. Flowers mainly in winter.

HABITAT/RANGE: Coastal heathland and open forest areas of Queensland, New South Wales, Victoria and Tasmania.

Scarlet Banksia *Banksia coccinea*

HEIGHT/ID: 5m. Multi-stemmed shrub with furry branches. Leaves are leathery to touch and oblong, can be 10cm long and 7cm wide, with some spikes on ends of leaves.

FLOWERS: Bright scarlet cylindrical spike up to 12cm long. Red styles tipped with a soft gold colour. Flowers from winter to summer.

HABITAT/RANGE: Light sandy soils and some gravel areas of south-west Western Australia.

Tennis Ball Banksia *Banksia laevigata*

HEIGHT/ID: 2m. A rather straggling shrub. Leaves are broad and linear, up to 10cm long with spikes on ends of leaves.

FLOWERS: Aptly named, the round flowers are the size of tennis balls and cream in colour. Flowers late spring to early summer.

HABITAT/RANGE: Restricted to a small area of southern Western Australia.

Woolly Banksia *Banksia baueri*

HEIGHT/ID: 4m. A thick and dense shrub. Leaves rigid and oblong, up to 15cm long and 2cm wide. They are evenly serrated with prickly margins and also veined. Also called Possum Banksia.

FLOWERS: When fully in flower the cones can be 24cm across and 20cm high. Colour resembles that of a teddy bear or possum. Flowers from winter into spring.

HABITAT/RANGE: Damp forest or woodland areas of Western Australia.

Hairpin Banksia *Banksia spinulosa*

HEIGHT/ID: 3m. Straggling but erect multi-stemmed shrub. Leaves 15cm long, narrow and linear with a prominent point and usually serrated edges.

FLOWERS: Small, tubular, cone-shaped flowers are bronze or honey coloured with black protruding styles on the cylindrical cone. Cones grow to 20cm long and about 6cm wide. Flowers from summer through to winter.

HABITAT/RANGE: Open forest country and most tableland areas of Queensland, New South Wales and Victoria.

Desert Banksia *Banksia ornata*

HEIGHT/ID: 2m. Well-rounded erect shrub, densely covered with limbs and leaves. Leaves tough in texture, up to 10cm long and 2.5cm wide, with serrated edges and a sharp point at tip.

FLOWERS: Plentiful yellow to bronze cylindrical flowers, up to 15cm long.

HABITAT/RANGE: Prefers desert, sandy soils and open forest, mainly in south-east South Australia and the south-west of Victoria.

Red Lantern Banksia *Banksia caleyi*

HEIGHT/ID: 2m. Erect shrub with fine bark on trunk and leaves scattered on the limbs. Leaves grow to 14cm long and have serrated edges.

FLOWERS: Flowers start off cream at the base then turn rich red; they hang down from the stem. Flowers from late spring to summer.

HABITAT/RANGE: Sandy soils in open woodlands and heath country of Western Australia.

Creeping Banksia *Banksia repens*

HEIGHT/ID: Prostrate shrub with erect leaves and many hairy horizontal branches which grow to 50cm long and 15cm wide.

FLOWERS: Pink-brown tubular cone-shaped flowers usually grow from ground-level; up to 15cm long and 6–7cm wide. Flowers from spring to early summer.

HABITAT/RANGE: Favours open sandy soils and heathlands, mainly in the Stirling Ranges of Western Australia.

Parrot Bush *Banksia sessilis*

HEIGHT/ID: 4m. Erect shrub. Leaves wedge-shaped, up to 5cm long and 3cm wide, with sharp prickles on the points.

FLOWERS: Pale yellow flowers in small terminal head which grows to 3cm long. These are surrounded by floral leaves and the short bracts are pale brown flowers. Flowers in spring.

HABITAT/RANGE: Common in jarrah forest and some coastal regions of Western Australia.

Golden Dryandra *Banksia nobilis*

HEIGHT/ID: 5m. Multi-branched shrub. Leaves up to 30cm long and 1.5cm wide with many small triangular sections on either side, dark green above and nearly white underneath.

FLOWERS: Orange to yellow flower-heads up to 7cm across, surrounded by floral leaves on short stem. Flowers from late winter.

HABITAT/RANGE: Woodlands in southern Western Australia.

Showy Dryandra *Banksia formosa*

HEIGHT/ID: 4–8m. Erect shrub or small tree. Branches covered with small hairs. Leaves narrow and linear and divided into many triangular lobes, edges lined with sharp needle-like thorns.

FLOWERS: Shiny yellow or orange with long hairy lobes and protruding styles, arranged in dense terminal head. Flowers in spring.

HABITAT/RANGE: Widespread in sandy heathlands of Western Australia.

Many-headed Dryandra *Banksia polycephala*

HEIGHT/ID: 4m. Tall and erect shrub. Leaves linear, up to 20cm long, recurved and well spaced with prickly lobes.

FLOWERS: Bright yellow heads up to 4cm across. Often many blooms on one branch. Flowers from winter.

HABITAT/RANGE: Woodlands and gravelly areas of south-west Western Australia.

Urchin Dryandra *Banksia undata*

HEIGHT/ID: 3m. Large and bushy shrub with hairy branches. Leaves egg-shaped and can be 10cm long and 6cm wide.

FLOWERS: Large golden flower-head has terminal heads, surrounded by clumps of floral leaves. Flowers winter to spring.

HABITAT/RANGE: Forest areas of south-west Western Australia.

Prickly Dryandra *Banksia falcata*

HEIGHT/ID: 4m. Erect loose shrub. Leaves up to 14cm long, alternated on stem, curled with long spines on edges. Branches have long brown hairs.

FLOWERS: From yellow to cream and faintly scented. Up to 40 flowers per stem. Flowers from winter to spring.

HABITAT/RANGE: A variety of habitats in south-west Western Australia.

Fuchsia Grevillea *Grevillea bipinnatifida*

HEIGHT/ID: 1.5m. Mainly a low and sprawling shrub, often prostrate. Limbs very hairy. Leaves rigid and prickly, growing to 20cm long and are divided into wedge shapes.

FLOWERS: Red flowers up to 15cm long with silky hair on outside. Flowers arranged in pendulous style, one side is spiky and resembles a spider.

HABITAT/RANGE: Harsh gravel and granite country in Western Australia.

Pink Pokers *Grevillea petrophiloides*

HEIGHT/ID: 2.4m. Tall and erect but spreading shrub. Leaves divided like 30cm-long needles.

FLOWERS: Pink to red cylindrical spike about 10cm long, sticky and with four curled back lobes.

HABITAT/RANGE: Prefers gravel or sandy soils in Queensland, Western Australia and Northern Territory.

Silky Oak Grevillea *Grevillea banksii*

HEIGHT/ID: 8m. Tall and spreading tree. Leaves divided, partly rounded and pointed. They can be 30cm long and are usually dark green.

FLOWERS: Usually cream-white, but can also be red or pink, they have a cylindrical spiked petal. Flowers from spring to summer.

HABITAT/RANGE: Widely distributed in coastal areas and open forests of Queensland.

Woolly Grevillea *Grevillea lanigera*

HEIGHT/ID: 2m. Mostly a rounded and hairy shrub. Leaves appear to be crowded on stem; they are linear, covered with soft hairs and can be up to 25cm long.

FLOWERS: Red flowers 6cm across with protruding styles and arranged in small clusters. Flowers can also be cream, green or pink. Flowers from spring to summer.

HABITAT/RANGE: Widespread in open woodland and gravelly or sandy areas of South Australia and Victoria.

82

Flame Grevillea *Grevillea eriostachya*

HEIGHT/ID: 2m. Very bushy shrub with stems that rise about 30cm above grey-green foliage. Leaf lobes very thin and up to 6cm long.

FLOWERS: Very colourful in flower. Greenish bud opens to a brilliant golden-yellow spike. A favourite with many nectar-loving birds. Flowers from spring to summer.

HABITAT/RANGE: Prefers dry sandy soils in Western Australia, Northern Territory and parts of South Australia.

Comb-leaf Grevillea *Grevillea pectinata*

HEIGHT/ID: 2m. Very erect shrub with divided pinnate leaves, which are loose, up to 3cm long and have a comb-like appearance.

FLOWERS: Usually deep red, but can be pink. They appear in clusters and follow no pattern on the shrub. Flowers in spring.

HABITAT/RANGE: Sandy loam or light gravel areas in southern Western Australia.

Mountain Grevillea *Grevillea alpina*

HEIGHT/ID: 1m. Sometimes this bush is prostrate, otherwise it is a low and spreading shrub and usually covered with hairy down. Leaves are soft, often crowded and dark green, up to 3cm long and 1cm wide.

FLOWERS: Usually red-orange, but can be green, yellow or pink, sometimes a combination of colours. Grampians form shown. Flowers from spring to summer.

HABITAT/RANGE: Favours sandy or open bush areas. Widespread in Victoria, occurs locally in New South Wales and South Australia.

Silver Grevillea *Grevillea parallela*

HEIGHT/ID: 10m. Tall shrub or tree with pendulous foliage. Leaves narrow and taper towards base, usually dull green above and covered with silky hair-veins on underside. Leaves may be divided into narrow lobes.

FLOWERS: Cream to white perfumed flowers are waxy, up to 10cm long, and crowded on cylindrical racemes. Flowers from mid-winter to summer.

HABITAT/RANGE: A variety of habitats in Northern Territory and Queensland.

Holly Grevillea *Grevillea aquifolium*

HEIGHT/ID: 4m. Can be prostrate, spreading or a tall shrub. Leaves up to 10cm long and to 4cm wide and can be oblong or ovate – they follow no pattern. They are often hairy, have some veins and can also be prickly.

FLOWERS: Colour varies – can be red, green or yellow. Racemes red, up to 5cm long and have no hairs. Flowers from spring to summer.

HABITAT/RANGE: Prefers light sandy open country in areas of Victoria and South Australia. One of eight species of grevillea in the Grampians.

Comb Grevillea *Grevillea huegelii*

HEIGHT/ID: 2.6m. A rigid, partly spreading and partly prostrate bush. Leaves stiff and divided into several pointed linear segments up to 2cm long and 2mm wide.

FLOWERS: Tubular and mainly red, sometimes pink and usually about 2.5cm long with four curled back petals. Flowers arranged in clusters. Flowers from spring to summer.

HABITAT/RANGE: Prefers light sandy soils and open bushland in areas of Western Australia, South Australia, Victoria and New South Wales.

White-plumed Grevillea *Grevillea leucopteris*

HEIGHT/ID: 3m. A very showy grevillea with many branches and pinnate leaves.

FLOWERS: White flowers hang on arched limbs and have a strong and unpleasant scent. Young buds covered with sticky pink bracts. Flowers from spring to summer.

HABITAT/RANGE: Sandy and heathland areas of Western Australia.

Grevillea sp. *Grevillea pinaster*

HEIGHT/ID: 4m. Trunk erect but looks straggling because of bushy branches which give woolly appearance. Leaves linear and silver-grey.

FLOWERS: Masses of deep pink or orange spider-like flowers appear in one-sided clusters which are up to 4cm long. Flowers winter to spring.

HABITAT/RANGE: Well-drained soil in open forest areas of south-west Western Australia.

Enfield Grevillea *Grevillea bedggoodiana*

HEIGHT/ID: 50cm. A spreading plant that is slightly prostrate. Leaves flat with sharp points along each edge, about 3cm across.

FLOWERS: Plum red or green flowers attached to the stem by short branches. Flowers can be single or in clusters. Flowers from spring to summer.

HABITAT/RANGE: Eucalypt forest in Enfield State Forest, Victoria.

Wickham's Grevillea *Grevillea wickhamii*

HEIGHT/ID: 4m. A very erect shrub. Leaves grey-green, flat, ovate, pointed and hairy, and up to 9cm long and 5cm wide.

FLOWERS: Red, orange or yellow flowers hang in clusters from main stalk. Flowers mainly in winter.

HABITAT/RANGE: Gravelly areas, limestone and spinifex country in Western Australia, Northern Territory and Queensland.

Long-style Grevillea *Grevillea longistyla*

HEIGHT/ID: 2.5m. Erect and open shrub. Branches silky, leaves linear and up to 25cm long.

FLOWERS: Red flowers in a loose cylindrical cluster. Racemes 10cm long, styles red and about 4cm long. Flowers from spring to summer.

HABITAT/RANGE: Sand plains, ridges and open forest areas of Queensland.

Coastal Hakea *Hakea clavata*

HEIGHT/ID: 2m. Spreading shrub with short brown branches. Leaves very succulent and slender.

FLOWERS: Rounded pale pink flowers in clusters about 3cm wide. Styles usually white and often smooth, can be 1cm or longer. Flowers mainly in winter.

HABITAT/RANGE: Coastal plains of south Western Australia.

Pincushion Hakea *Hakea laurina*

HEIGHT/ID: 3m. Spreading shrub with many branches, which at times are pendulous. Pointed leathery leaves are lance-shaped with prominent veins, up to 18cm long and 2.5cm wide.

FLOWERS: Light cream to begin, then turn crimson in a densely rounded ball of about 6cm. Cream to white styles protrude from centre of ball, these can be 2–3cm in length. Flowers in winter.

HABITAT/RANGE: Widespread on coastal plains of southern Western Australia.

Red Pokers Hakea *Hakea bucculenta*

HEIGHT/ID: 2m. An open and erect shrub. Leaves are linear and can be 20cm long and 2cm wide; they are flat and leathery to touch, with one central vein and a pointed tip.

FLOWERS: Red flowers in long spikes with racemes up to 18cm long. The style can be 2cm and slightly curved. Flowers from winter.

HABITAT/RANGE: Moist sandy soils and some areas of gravel surface in lower Western Australia.

Cauliflower Hakea *Hakea corymbosa*

HEIGHT/ID: 2m. A round-shaped shrub with short, hairy branches. Leaves are narrow and pointed, up to 8cm long and 8mm wide.

FLOWERS: Green to cream in colour, with dense clusters about 2.5cm across. They almost cover the shrub and the upper leaf axils are cream and smooth. Flowers in late winter to spring.

HABITAT/RANGE: Coastal areas, sand plains and mallee country in southern Western Australia.

Sea Urchin Hakea *Hakea petiolaris*

HEIGHT/ID: 2m. Erect shrub. Grey-green leaves are egg-shaped with pointed tip and prominent veins; up to 12cm long and 6cm wide.

FLOWERS: Cream at first then gradually turn pink to purple. The flowers grow to 5cm wide and are often found on the older wood or stalks. Flowers winter to autumn.

HABITAT/RANGE: Coastal areas and heathlands of Western Australia.

Snail Hakea *Hakea cristata*

HEIGHT/ID: 2m. A small, erect scrub. Leaves alternate along the trunk; they are up to 8cm long, egg-shaped, flat and have prickly edges.

FLOWERS: Slightly scented white flowers about 2cm across grow from the stem or trunk.

HABITAT/RANGE: Scrubland, sandy soils and granite outcrops in an area near Perth, Western Australia.

King Hakea *Hakea cucullata*

HEIGHT/ID: 4m. Open-branched shrub, with cupped, heart-shaped leaves up to 8cm across, which support the racemes of flowers.

FLOWERS: Buds enclosed by a broad silky bract. Flowers can be either red, pink or white. Flowers from late autumn to spring.

HABITAT/RANGE: Prefers the open heathlands of southern Western Australia.

Grass-leaved Hakea *Hakea multilineata*

HEIGHT/ID: 4.5m. Tall and erect shrub or small tree. Light green leaves are broad and linear, up to 20cm long and 1.5cm wide.

FLOWERS: From deep pink to red, in spikes up to 4cm long. Flowers from winter to spring.

HABITAT/RANGE: Grows in any type of soil and mainly in the south-west of Western Australia.

Long-leaved Petrophile *Petrophile longifolia*

HEIGHT/ID: 40cm. A ground-hugging plant with slender leaves.

FLOWERS: Silky flower-heads up to 6cm across are surrounded by many small pointed bracts. Flowers can be orange or yellow. Flowers from late spring to early summer.

HABITAT/RANGE: Prefers gravelly to limestone country and heathlands of Western Australia.

Hairy Jugflower *Adenanthos barbiger*

HEIGHT/ID: 45cm. Small erect multi-stemmed shrub. Flat green leaves up to 5cm long.

FLOWERS: Bright red, up to 4cm in diameter, with curled stamen at tip of flower. Flowers in spring.

HABITAT/RANGE: Common in sandy soils of south-west Western Australia.

Chittick *Lambertia inermis*

HEIGHT/ID: 3m. Straggling plant. Leaves are egg-shaped and pointed at tip.

FLOWERS: Can be orange or yellow. Flower-heads usually in clumps of seven. Styles up to 4cm long. Will flower at any time of the year if conditions suit.

HABITAT/RANGE: Open heathlands and gravelly areas near the south coast of Western Australia.

Common Smokebush *Conospermum stoechadis*

HEIGHT/ID: 1.5m. Erect and dome-shaped shrub, with many branches giving the plant a dense appearance. Slender leaves grow to 10cm long and are pointed at tip.

FLOWERS: Whitish-grey, from a distance can appear to be a shade of blue. They are woolly and tubular, growing to 8mm long. Flowers from spring.

HABITAT/RANGE: Open woodland and gravelly heathlands of Western Australia.

Cut-leaf Guinea Flower *Hibbertia cuneiformis*

HEIGHT/ID: 3m. Erect and bushy shrub. Leaves oblong and up to 4cm long, with some small prickles near the tip.

FLOWERS: The bright yellow flowers are prominent, 3–4cm across. Stamens are clustered into five bundles. Flowers from spring.

HABITAT/RANGE: Coastal districts of south-west Western Australia.

Spreading Guinea Flower *Hibbertia procumbens*

HEIGHT/ID: Prostrate to 40cm. A twiggy shrub with narrow stalks. Mainly prostrate and can spread to over 1m in diameter. Leaves small and dark with pointed tips and can be up to 2cm long.

FLOWERS: Bright yellow flowers bloom in great numbers at the ends of branches. Each flower has five petals and can be up to 10cm in diameter. Flowers from spring to summer.

HABITAT/RANGE: Prefers the open bushland areas and heathlands of Victoria, New South Wales and south-east Queensland.

Common Popflower *Glischrocaryon aureum*

HEIGHT/ID: 70cm. A tufted herb perennial with a very tough root system but no leaf system.

FLOWERS: A mass of yellow flowers hanging down in loose clusters from the numerous slender stems. Flowers in spring.

HABITAT/RANGE: Grows in a variety of soils and conditions. Most often found in the drier areas of Victoria, South Australia and Western Australia.

Pink Mulla Mulla *Ptilotus exaltatus*

HEIGHT/ID: 1m. Upright perennial herb. Leaves oblong and lanceolate; they can grow to 20cm long and 7cm wide with a thick tip at the end.

FLOWERS: Cone-shaped and lengthening to a cylindrical point; up to 25cm long and 5cm wide. Flowers deep pink and covered in a mass of silky hairs, but not on the tip of the flower. Flowers from winter to spring.

HABITAT/RANGE: Widespread across the arid inland of all mainland states. Flowers well after rain and appears to have no soil preference.

Black Bluebush *Maireana pyramidata*

HEIGHT/ID: 1m. Mostly a dome-shaped shrub. Stem can be hairy or smooth. Leaves very succulent and slender.

FLOWERS: Small and solitary greenish-yellow flowers with a shiny appearance. Flowers in spring.

HABITAT/RANGE: Widespread in the dry inland areas of all states of mainland Australia.

Batchelor's Buttons *Gomphrena canescens*

HEIGHT/ID: 75cm. Erect-branched shrub. Leaves hairy, linear and sword-shaped, up to 6cm long and 5cm wide.

FLOWERS: Globular and papery, up to 6cm across. Can be pale pink, pink or red. Flowers in autumn and winter.

HABITAT/RANGE: Common among native grasses and along roadsides in Northern Territory, Western Australia and Queensland.

Tall Sundew *Drosera auriculata*

HEIGHT/ID: 30cm. Insectivorous, mostly erect herb. Height variable. Leaves nearly circular and form a flat rosette. Long hairs on leaves have sticky droplets at tips to trap insects.

FLOWERS: White or pink, usually 1.5cm across. Sepals hairless. Flowers from winter to spring.

HABITAT/RANGE: Common in damp areas and moist sandy bushland in South Australia, Victoria, Tasmania, New South Wales and south-east Queensland.

Grampians Bauera *Bauera sessiliflora*

HEIGHT/ID: 2m. Tall and erect bushy shrub with hairy branches. Leaves divided into three oblong leaflets, up to 2.5cm.

FLOWERS: Magenta or pink with five small open petals and usually crowded into a small cluster. Stalkless with numerous black-tipped stamens. Flowers in spring.

HABITAT/RANGE: Sheltered sandy low areas or swamps. Endemic to the Grampians of Victoria.

Pink-bells *Tetratheca ciliata*

HEIGHT/ID: 90cm. A small and slender shrub with a number of hairy ridged branches. Leaves alternate and fringed with hairs.

FLOWERS: From lilac to pink or red, seldom white, and 2.5cm wide. Always has dark brown centre, either eight or ten stamens and four spreading petals. Flowers mainly in spring.

HABITAT/RANGE: Grows in most sandy soils, heathlands and forest regions of New South Wales, Queensland, South Australia and Tasmania.

Upside-down Plant *Leptosema chambersii*

HEIGHT/ID: 70cm. A small leafless shrub with a tangle of grey-green stems.

FLOWERS: The long red flowers have red stamens. They grow at the base of the plant, resting on the soil. Flowers in winter.

HABITAT/RANGE: Desert areas of Northern Territory, South Australia and Western Australia.

Green Birdflower *Crotalaria cunninghamii*

HEIGHT/ID: 2m. Erect shrub with high branches. Stems feel leathery. Leaves are egg-shaped, hairy, velvet to touch and grow up to 8cm long.

FLOWERS: Pea-shaped and usually green, sometimes yellow. They are streaked with thin black lines and grow to 4cm long. Racemes can be over 20cm long. Flowers from winter to spring.

HABITAT/RANGE: Grows in sandy inland habitats in South Australia, Western Australia, Northern Territory, Queensland and New South Wales.

Running Postman *Kennedia prostrata*

HEIGHT/ID: Prostrate. A creeping shrub that can cover up to 5m in area. Leaves formed of three leaflets, circular and partly egg-shaped, up to 3cm long.

FLOWERS: Bright red and pea-shaped with small yellow centre. Can grow individually or in pairs. Flowers from winter to spring.

HABITAT/RANGE: In a variety of soils and conditions, including open forests, heathlands and sandy-clay areas in Western Australia, South Australia, Victoria, Tasmania and New South Wales.

Cockies' Tongues *Templetonia retusa*

HEIGHT/ID: 1.5m. Mainly erect shrub, but can be prostrate, with very rigid branches. Grey-green leaves are often leathery, oblong and broaden towards tip.

FLOWERS: Mainly deep red, but can be white or pink-purple. Up to 4cm long, pea-shaped with a curled-back petal and a long and narrow keel arranged in a small auxiliary cluster. Flowers winter to spring.

HABITAT/RANGE: Sandy soils, open heathlands, forests and mallee country of South Australia and Western Australia.

Sturt's Desert Pea *Swainsona formosa*

HEIGHT/ID: Prostrate. Spreading annual or perennial plant with thick upright stems covered in fine hairs. Grey-green leaves up to 15cm long and divided into narrow 3cm-long oblong leaflets.

FLOWERS: Bright red pea-shaped flower up to 8cm long. Pointed with erect racemes and a large raised glossy black spot at the base. Flowers at almost any time after rain. Floral emblem of South Australia.

HABITAT/RANGE: Dry inland areas of all mainland states except Victoria.

Matted Bush-pea *Pultenaea pedunculata*

HEIGHT/ID: Prostrate form. Habitat varies greatly with this plant, often the prostrate stems will take root. Leaves are crowded; they are narrow and grow to 1cm long.

FLOWERS: Small yellow flowers on thread-like stems, can be up to 2cm long and are conspicuous in the bush. Flowers can be orange or yellow. Flowers in spring.

HABITAT/RANGE: Dry bushland areas of Victoria, South Australia, New South Wales and Tasmania.

Dwarf Wedge-pea *Gompholobium ecostatum*

HEIGHT/ID: 30cm. Erect or sometimes a spreading shrub. Leaves have three linear leaflets that grow to 1cm long.

FLOWERS: Pea-shaped, varying from deep apricot to red with a yellow centre. Flower can be solitary or in pairs. Flowers from spring to summer.

HABITAT/RANGE: Sandy soils and open forest areas of Victoria and South Australia.

Common Wedge-pea *Gompholobium huegelii*

HEIGHT/ID: 30cm. A herbaceous and scrambling plant. Leaves have three linear leaflets up to 10cm long and 1cm wide; these are on the stems of the plant.

FLOWERS: Yellow pea-shaped blooms very uniform in size and colour. Flowers in spring.

HABITAT/RANGE: Prefers the sandy and gravelly areas and open bushland regions of Tasmania. Victoria and New South Wales.

Narrow-leaf Bitter-pea *Daviesia leptophylla*

HEIGHT/ID: 2m. A broom-like shrub. Oval-shaped leaves up to 6cm long and bitter to taste.

FLOWERS: Golden-yellow, sometimes yellow and brown, pea flowers. Flowers occupy very dense racemes. Flowers late spring to summer.

HABITAT/RANGE: Open bushland and forest areas of Victoria, New South Wales and Tasmania.

Common Flat-pea *Platylobium obtusangulum*

HEIGHT/ID: 1m. Erect, spreading shrub with wiry branches. Leaves triangular and pointed, up to 3cm long.

FLOWERS: Pea-shaped flowers are orange-yellow with red-brown centres and overlapping bracts. Some are single, others in clumps of two or three. Flowers in spring.

HABITAT/RANGE: Common in heathland and open forest areas of South Australia, Victoria and Tasmania.

Showy Parrot-pea *Dillwynia sericea*

HEIGHT/ID: 1m. Tall erect shrub, stem usually covered with white silky hairs, more often when plant is young. Linear leaves grow to 2cm.

FLOWERS: Pea-shaped flowers about 1.5cm across and golden-yellow, or can be orange with some red markings. Flowers are often in pairs on the upper leaf axils. Flowers in winter and spring.

HABITAT/RANGE: Widespread in heathlands and open forest areas of southern South Australia, Victoria, Tasmania, New South Wales and south-east Queensland.

Swan River Pea *Brachysema celsianum*

HEIGHT/ID: 1.5m. A small spreading shrub which will climb if possible. Stems have silvery hairs. Leaves sword-like in appearance, dark green and smooth, can grow to 10cm.

FLOWERS: Pea-shaped and red, grow to about 2.5cm long and are usually solitary, sometimes in a cluster of two or three. Flowers from winter to spring.

HABITAT/RANGE: Areas of mallee scrubland in Western Australia.

Fire Bush *Senna pleurocarpa*

HEIGHT/ID: 1.5m. Very sprawling and hairless shrub. It will also sucker if conditions suit. Leaves are divided and up to 17cm long.

FLOWERS: Yellow flowers usually 1.6cm across; they are erect and have spike-like racemes. Flowers at any time of the year when conditions suit.

HABITAT/RANGE: In the sandy areas of all mainland Australia except Victoria.

Mudgee Wattle *Acacia spectabilis*

HEIGHT/ID: 2m. Erect shrub, stem often hangs in a drooping fashion and covered with thick hairs. Blue-green leaves are divided, oblong and pointed at tip.

FLOWERS: Golden-yellow, the globular heads are on long racemes which can measure 15cm. Flowers from winter to spring.

HABITAT/RANGE: In areas of forest and bushland of north-east New South Wales and south-east Queensland.

West Wyalong Wattle *Acacia cardiophylla*

HEIGHT/ID: 3m. A bushy shrub with finely divided, soft green fern-like foliage; each leaflet is about 2cm long. Has long arching branches that become covered with flowers.

FLOWERS: The branches are a mass of spiky yellow balls in spring. Flowers from winter to spring.

HABITAT/RANGE: A mallee country species of New South Wales.

Sydney Golden Wattle *Acacia longifolia*

HEIGHT/ID: 8m. Erect and spreading tree. Has flattened stalks that double as leaves (phyllodes); these can be up to 20cm long.

FLOWERS: Golden yellow in a spike up to 20cm long. Flowers from winter to spring.

HABITAT/RANGE: Coastal areas and mountain ranges of New South Wales, Victoria and south-east South Australia.

Witchetty Bush *Acacia kempeana*

HEIGHT/ID: 3m. Erect and a spreading shrub, the phyllodes are flattened and slightly curled, growing to 10cm long and 1.5cm wide; small veins run through and the tip is rounded.

FLOWERS: Golden-yellow flowers in spikes and about 3cm long. Flowers from winter to spring.

HABITAT/RANGE: Widespread in the dry areas of Queensland, South Australia, Western Australia and Northern Territory.

Queensland Silver Wattle *Acacia podalyriifolia*

HEIGHT/ID: 4 m. Erect shrub, stems often hairy. Phyllodes flat, almost egg-shaped and up to 3cm long and 2cm wide; usually silver-grey.

FLOWERS: Golden-yellow flowers in a globular head, set on slender stalk on stem. Flowers from winter to spring.

HABITAT/RANGE: Mainly coastal areas of New South Wales and Queensland; also locally in Victoria and Western Australia.

Flat Wattle *Acacia glaucoptera*

HEIGHT/ID: 1m. Well branched and rounded shrub. Unusual flat grey leaf-like stems overlap continuously in zigzagged pattern. New growth often red or bronze.

FLOWERS: Yellow balls emerge from central stem during spring.

HABITAT/RANGE: Well-drained areas of forest and bush in Western Australia and New South Wales.

Grey Mulga *Acacia brachybotrya*

HEIGHT/ID: 1m. A spreading shrub, the stem is covered with small hairs. Phyllodes green, egg-shaped and up to 4cm long with rounded tip.

FLOWERS: Bright yellow with globular heads. Can be in clusters or sometimes single-headed on the stem. Flowers from winter to spring.

HABITAT/RANGE: The dry inland regions of mainly the mallee areas of New South Wales, Victoria and South Australia.

Sword-leaf Wattle *Acacia gladiiformis*

HEIGHT/ID: 3m. Evergreen. Stem is shrub-like with angular branches. Phyllodes are leathery and curved, rigid and narrow.

FLOWERS: Flowers are golden balls which occur in loose sprays on the stems. Flowers in spring.

HABITAT/RANGE: Thrives in most soils in the New South Wales area.

Painted Featherflower *Verticordia picta*

HEIGHT/ID: 1m. Small shrub. Leaves long and narrow and usually grow to 1cm.

FLOWERS: Pink or purple, up to 1.2cm across with rounded petals and feather-like sepals. They are profuse and grow in loose clusters. Flowers in spring.

HABITAT/RANGE: Open bushland areas of southern and western Western Australia.

Yellow Featherflower *Verticordia chrysantha*

HEIGHT/ID: 80cm. Small erect shrub. Leaves linear, slender and pointed at tip.

FLOWERS: Yellow, up to 1.5cm across. Grow profusely in loose clusters. Feather-like petals heavily fringed. Flowers in spring.

HABITAT/RANGE: Heathlands and sand plains of Western Australia.

Woolly Featherflower *Verticordia monadelpha*

HEIGHT/ID: 1m. Thick and bushy shrub. Leaves up to 3cm long but not seen when bush in flower.

FLOWERS: Mass of feathery pink to lilac-purple flowers, up to 8cm across. Flowers mainly in spring.

HABITAT/RANGE: Clay and sandy soils in Geraldton area of Western Australia.

Roe's Featherflower *Verticordia roei*

HEIGHT/ID: 45cm. Small tightly cropped shrub, no leaves or limbs visible when in flower.

FLOWERS: Mainly tight clusters of white flowers, about 1cm across. All of the flowers open simultaneously. Flowers from early spring to early summer.

HABITAT/RANGE: Light sandy soils and gravelly areas of southern Western Australia.

Verticordia sp. *Verticordia etheliana*

HEIGHT/ID: 30cm. Small perennial herb. Leaves 2–3cm long, flat and smooth and almost round.

FLOWERS: Brilliant red flowers grow from stems, they have long tips to 4–5cm long and a feathery rosette of petals. Flowers in spring.

HABITAT/RANGE: Sandy areas and open heaths in Geraldton area of Western Australia.

Verticordia sp. *Verticordia oculata*

HEIGHT/ID: 70cm. Low-growing, sprawling shrub. Several stems emerge from the one main plant.

FLOWERS: Flowers and stem leaves all circular, with white margin attached directly to the stem; flowers up to 1cm long and have to 14 white lobes. Flowers grouped like a spreading arrangement near the upper area of the stem. Flowers in summer.

HABITAT/RANGE: Sandy heathlands in Geraldton area of Western Australia.

Swamp Paperbark *Melaleuca ericifolia*

HEIGHT/ID: 6m. Small tree or shrub with greyish trunk. Alternate leaves can be 1–2cm long – they are narrow, linear and often the tip is curved at the end.

FLOWERS: Usually white to off-white, rarely any other color. Flowers crowded in heads or sometimes in short spikes up to 2.5cm long; these grow into leafy shoots. Stamens creamy-white. Flowers from spring to summer.

HABITAT/RANGE: Heathlands and sandy areas in New South Wales, Victoria and Tasmania.

Bracelet Honey-myrtle *Melaleuca armillaris*

HEIGHT/ID: 5m. Shrub or small tree with firm bark and grey trunk. Leaves linear, up to 2.5cm long and 1cm wide, with pointed tips.

FLOWERS: Cylinder-shaped white flowers. Flowers from spring to summer.

HABITAT/RANGE: Widespread over heathlands and tablelands of New South Wales, Victoria, South Australia and areas of Tasmania and south-west Western Australia.

Melaleuca sp. *Melaleuca thymoides*

HEIGHT/ID: 2m. A small shrub with sword-like leaves which are 1–3cm long.

FLOWERS: Small yellow flower-heads, mainly at ends of stiff limbs. Flowers in spring and summer.

HABITAT/RANGE: Sandy areas and open heathlands of south-west Western Australia.

Chenille Honey-myrtle *Melaleuca huegelii*

HEIGHT/ID: 3m. Shrub with triangular leaves, which are small and crowded against the stems. Makes a good windbreak – can be cut to form windbreaks if needed.

FLOWERS: Flowers in spikes up to 10cm long. Red petals often hidden when flowering by pink or white stamen bundles. Flowers late spring to early summer.

HABITAT/RANGE: Coastal and limestone areas of Western Australia.

Corky Honey-myrtle *Melaleuca suberosa*

HEIGHT/ID: 70cm. Very unusual shrub with linear leaves up to 1cm long. Has thick corky bark on trunk.

FLOWERS: Flowers appear to emerge through the bark along the length of a stem and can be lilac, pink or red. Flowers spring to summer.

HABITAT/RANGE: Sandy heathlands in southern Western Australia.

Totem Poles *Melaleuca decussata*

HEIGHT/ID: 5m. Erect shrub. Pointed bluish-green leaves are opposite each other, sometimes crowded on stem.

FLOWERS: Usually pale lilac and has five lobes with numerous protruding stamens all arranged in cylindrical hairy spikes. Flowers from spring to summer.

HABITAT/RANGE: Rocky areas and sandy flats, often near water or swamps, in Victoria and South Australia.

Scarlet Honey-myrtle *Melaleuca fulgens*

HEIGHT/ID: 2m. Erect and sprawling shrub. Leaves sword-shaped, pointed at tip and up to 3cm long.

FLOWERS: Usually red, sometimes orange or pink. Spikes up to 5cm long and 4cm wide. Flowers from spring to summer.

HABITAT/RANGE: Usually associated with wheat-growing areas of Western Australia.

Wiry Honey-myrtle *Melaleuca filifolia*

HEIGHT/ID: 2m. Erect shrub. Thin slender leaves are up to 3cm long and 15cm wide, slightly curved and pointed. Formerly known as *M. nematophylla*.

FLOWERS: Purple-mauve with golden anthers. Rounded terminal flower-heads about 5cm in diameter. Spring flowering.

HABITAT/RANGE: Open sand plains of Western Australia.

Wilson's Honey-myrtle *Melaleuca wilsonii*

HEIGHT/ID: 1.2m. Dense shrub, can be prostrate at times. Narrow pointed leaves have a citrus scent when crushed.

FLOWERS: Usually pink-lilac, sometimes white. Flowers bloom along the branches in dense clusters. Flowers from spring to summer.

HABITAT/RANGE: Semi-arid areas of Victoria and South Australia.

Prickly Paperbark *Melaleuca styphelioides*

HEIGHT/ID: 20m. A small shrub with papery bark. Bright green leaves are about 2cm long, slightly twisted and egg-shaped with a sharp tip.

FLOWERS: Profuse white flowers in cylindrical clumps up to 3cm long. Flowers from spring to summer.

HABITAT/RANGE: Coastal areas and swampland mainly in New South Wales, also locally in Victoria and south-east Queensland.

Prickly-leaved Paperbark *Melaleuca nodosa*

HEIGHT/ID: 1.2m. Erect shrub with papery bark on trunk. Leaves slender, sharply pointed and rigid, up to 3cm long.

FLOWERS: Pale yellow with globular flower-heads up to 1.5cm across. Flowers from spring to summer.

HABITAT/RANGE: Widespread on coastal and sandy heathlands of Queensland and New South Wales.

Broombush *Melaleuca uncinata*

HEIGHT/ID: 2m. Erect and multi-stemmed shrub with papery bark on trunk. Slender leaves grow to 6cm long; tips pointed and slightly recurved.

FLOWERS: Flowers usually pale yellow or light cream and grow in globular heads which are about 1.5cm across and often terminal. Flowers from winter to spring.

HABITAT/RANGE: Dry inland regions of all mainland states. Often grows among the mallee eucalypt trees.

Melaleuca sp. *Melaleuca pentagona*

HEIGHT/ID: 3m. Erect shrub. Leaves are needle-like and pointed, up to 2cm long.

FLOWERS: Pink and in tight clusters on the stems, with pale golden tips on ends of flower-heads.

HABITAT/RANGE: Sandy heathlands and open forest areas in Western Australia.

Granite Honey-myrtle *Melaleuca elliptica*

HEIGHT/ID: 2.5m. Erect shrub. Grey bark is slippery and papery. Leaves 1.5cm long, flat with rounded tip.

FLOWERS: Red cylindrical spikes up to 8cm long and 5cm across on older stems. Flowers from spring to summer.

HABITAT/RANGE: Granite areas of southern Western Australia.

Rough Honey-myrtle *Melaleuca scabra*

HEIGHT/ID: 1–2m. Small spreading shrub. Leaves 1cm long and linear with very prominent point on tip.

FLOWERS: Deep pink to purple in terminal heads about 1cm across. Flowers from spring to summer.

HABITAT/RANGE: Widespread in heath and forest areas of Western Australia.

Graceful Honey-myrtle *Melaleuca radula*

HEIGHT/ID: 1.5m. Spreading shrub. Leaves long and narrow, up to 5cm long, pointed at tip and glandular.

FLOWERS: Pink or purple spikes up to 2.5cm long on short stem. Flowers from winter to spring.

HABITAT/RANGE: Coastal areas and open heathlands of Western Australia.

Showy Honey-myrtle *Melaleuca nesophila*

HEIGHT/ID: 2m. Bush-shaped shrub with papery bark on trunk. Leathery leaves 2cm long and oblong with rounded tip which may have a small point.

FLOWERS: Mauve to purple globular terminal head up to 3cm across. Flowers from winter to spring.

HABITAT/RANGE: Sandy coastal regions of Western Australia.

Robin Red-breast Bush *Melaleuca lateritia*

HEIGHT/ID: 1.5m. Multi-stemmed and open bush. Leaves thin, flat, up to 2cm long and pointed at tip.

FLOWERS: Orange to red 8cm-long spikes on short stems, usually on old wood. Flowers from spring to summer.

HABITAT/RANGE: Widespread in the mallee areas and heathland of Western Australia.

Green-flowered Paperbark *Melaleuca viridiflora*

HEIGHT/ID: 6m. Small tree with grey to cream trunks. Trunk very fibrous and bark in layers. Dull dark green leaves are broad, oval, flat, stiff, smooth and 15cm long.

FLOWERS: Usually pale greenish-yellow, can also be red. Dense cylindrical flower spikes, often in small groups. Flowers mainly in spring.

HABITAT/RANGE: Grows well in most soils, but prefers heavy clay, in Northern Territory, Queensland and north-east Western Australia.

Violet Kunzea   *Kunzea parvifolia*

HEIGHT/ID: 2.5m. Tall and erect shrub, slender in appearance with wiry branches. Dull green leaves small and stalkless, oblong, spear-like and curled with black tips; can be 4mm long and 1mm wide. Small glands on each leaf.

FLOWERS: Pinkish flowers 4–5mm wide with five small lobes and numerous long stamens. Small terminal heads are about 10cm wide.

HABITAT/RANGE: Elevated areas of New South Wales, Queensland and Victoria.

Baxter's Kunzea *Kunzea baxteri*

HEIGHT/ID: 1.5m. Spreading shrub with many stems. Leaves linear and oblong, up to 1.5cm long and often edged with tiny white hairs.

FLOWERS: Usually deep red. Dense cylindrical spikes about 2.5cm long are prominent. Stamens can be 10cm long and tipped with white or cream. Spring flowering.

HABITAT/RANGE: Granite country and coastal areas of southern Western Australia.

Tick Bush *Kunzea ambigua*

HEIGHT/ID: To 3m. Spreading shrub. Dark green leaves are narrow, pointed at tip and up to 1cm long.

FLOWERS: About 1.5cm wide and nearly always white. Stamens white and longer than petals. Flowers in spring.

HABITAT/RANGE: Coastal areas and heathlands of Tasmania, Victoria and New South Wales.

Pink Bottlebrush *Beaufortia schaueri*

HEIGHT/ID: 1m. Small-branched shrub. Leaves narrow, linear, pointed at tip, up to 3cm long and crowded.

FLOWERS: Can be lilac or pink. Flower-heads rounded and about 2cm across. Flowers at ends of short lateral branches. Flowers from winter to spring.

HABITAT/RANGE: Sandy heathlands and gravelly areas of southern Western Australia.

Stirling Range Bottlebrush *Beaufortia heterophylla*

HEIGHT/ID: 1m. Small-leaved and twiggy shrub. Leaves very hair-like in appearance; can grow to 10cm long.

FLOWERS: Flowers bright scarlet or purplish-red. Flower spikes clustered along branches. Prominent stamens up to 2.5cm long. Flowers winter to spring.

HABITAT/RANGE: Gravelly soil, open woodlands and heath country of north-east Western Australia.

Ravensthorpe Bottlebrush *Beaufortia orbifolia*

HEIGHT/ID: 3m. Small shrub. Leaves up to 2cm long. Small woody fruits crowded in spikes along stems.

FLOWERS: Flower spikes up to 4cm in diameter; they are bicoloured at first, then turn deep red. Flowers from winter to early summer.

HABITAT/RANGE: Open forest areas and roadsides of southern Western Australia.

Sand Bottlebrush *Beaufortia squarrosa*

HEIGHT/ID: 2m. Erect and spreading shrub. Leaves usually in pairs and can be 5cm long.

FLOWERS: Usually bright red, sometimes orange-yellow, in tufted spikes up to 3cm long. Flowers from spring to autumn.

HABITAT/RANGE: Sandy plains and heathlands of Western Australia.

Swamp Bottlebrush *Beaufortia sparsa*

HEIGHT/ID: 1.2m. Erect, open, spreading shrub. Leaves crowded and scattered along branch; they are egg-shaped with a pointed tip and some have curved-back margins.

FLOWERS: Red to orange cylindrical spikes up to 7cm long. Stamens wide and drooping. Flowers in summer.

HABITAT/RANGE: Swampy areas of sand plains and heathlands of south-west Western Australia.

Lemon Bottlebrush *Callistemon pallidus*

HEIGHT/ID: 3m. Stiff and erect shrub. Young growth usually has silky hairs on branches. Leaves stiff, leathery, narrow, pointed and up to 7cm long and 2cm wide.

FLOWERS: Cream to greenish-yellow spikes up to 7cm long and 3.5cm wide. Numerous long protruding stamens arranged in cylindrical spikes up to 9cm long. Flowers from spring to summer.

HABITAT/RANGE: Damp water courses and sandy heathlands of Tasmania, Victoria, New South Wales and south-east Queensland.

Scarlet Bottlebrush *Callistemon rugulosus*

HEIGHT/ID: 4m. Spreading and very branching shrub with some prickles on trunk. Leaves alternate and are narrow, sharply pointed and up to 8cm long. Oil glands in leaves are prominent.

FLOWERS: Bright red with numerous yellow-tipped stamens arranged through the cylindrical flower spike. Flowers in spring.

HABITAT/RANGE: Sandy to swampy soils in mallee and open forest land of Victoria and South Australia.

Wallum Bottlebrush *Callistemon pachyphyllus*

HEIGHT/ID: 1.5m. Spreading and open shrub. Thick, dull green leaves are narrow with pointed tip; up to 9cm long and 1cm wide.

FLOWERS: Bright red or green flower spikes 10cm long and 6cm wide. Flowers from spring to summer.

HABITAT/RANGE: Damp sandy areas of New South Wales and Queensland.

Stiff Bottlebrush *Callistemon rigidus*

HEIGHT/ID: 2.5m. Erect and a vigorous shrub. Young growth has silky hairs on stems. Leaves are linear with pointed tips; up to 7cm long.

FLOWERS: Red spiky flowers up to 10cm long and 6cm wide. Flowers from spring to summer.

HABITAT/RANGE: Coastal regions of New South Wales.

Dwarf Bottlebrush *Callistemon subulatus*

HEIGHT/ID: 1.8m. Small spreading shrub with arching branches. Leaves linear with very pointed tips, partly cyclindrical and up to 5cm long.

FLOWERS: Red spikes up to 8cm long and 5cm wide, often in clusters at ends of branches. Flowers from spring to summer.

HABITAT/RANGE: Coastal and some tableland areas of New South Wales and Victoria.

Prickly Bottlebrush *Callistemon brachyandrus*

HEIGHT/ID: 5m. Tall and erect spreading shrub. Leaves stiff, needle-sharp, pointed and grooved.

FLOWERS: Orange to red with five small lobes and numerous 1cm-long yellow-tipped stamens. Cylindrical spikes 3–5cm long. Flowers from spring.

HABITAT/RANGE: Creek beds and open forest areas of New South Wales, Victoria and South Australia.

Oldfield's Darwinia *Darwinia oldfieldii*

HEIGHT/ID: 1m. Small shrub with numerous short stems. Leaves mainly oblong; margins fringed and usually recurved.

FLOWERS: Deep red, often 10 or more flower-heads with long styles and very short bracts. Flowers from winter to spring.

HABITAT/RANGE: Mainly in Murchison River district of Western Australia.

Geraldton Wax *Chamelaucium uncinatum*

HEIGHT/ID: 1m. Very erect shrub with many long, slender branches. Leaves scented and linear with hairless tip and hooked point.

FLOWERS: Small terminal clusters. Open-petalled, 2.5cm across with wax-like appearance. Can be white, mauve or pink. Flowers from winter to spring.

HABITAT/RANGE: Sandplains and open areas, usually north of Perth in Kalbarri district.

Turkey Bush *Calytrix exstipulata*

HEIGHT/ID: 3m. Erect and bushy. Stems short and numerous. Three-sided leaves are long and crowded on stem.

FLOWERS: Deep pink and star-like. Can be white or pale pink to purple. Flowers profusely in clusters from autumn to winter.

HABITAT/RANGE: Woodland and open forest country in tropical regions of Queensland, Northern Territory and Western Australia.

Shiny Tea-tree *Leptospermum nitidum*

HEIGHT/ID: 3m. Erect and spreading shrub. Shiny green leaves are 7cm long, knife-shaped and pointed at tip.

FLOWERS: 3cm across with five separate white lobes around a green central disc and surrounded by many stamens. Flowers from spring to summer.

HABITAT/RANGE: Coastal areas and heathlands of Victoria and Tasmania.

Lilac Hibiscus *Alyogyne huegelii*

HEIGHT/ID: 2m. Erect shrub with rigid hairy branches. Leaves up to 7cm long and divided; lobes irregularly shaped and hairy on both sides.

FLOWERS: Lilac to pink, rarely white. Up to 12cm wide with five overlapping petals. Centre has yellow, star-like protruding style. Flowers spring to summer.

HABITAT/RANGE: Variety of habitats in South Australia and Western Australia.

Yellow Hibiscus *Hibiscus panduriformis*

HEIGHT/ID: 1.2m. Erect and open shrub; stems very hairy. Leaves egg-shaped with slight toothing and up to 9cm long and 8cm wide. Grey-green on top, much paler underneath.

FLOWERS: Solitary yellow flower with maroon centre, up to 12cm across. Flowers at any time of year when conditions suit.

HABITAT/RANGE: Clay-pan areas and savanna woodlands in Queensland, Northern Territory and Western Australia.

Sturt's Desert Rose *Gossypium sturtianum*

HEIGHT/ID: 2m. Dense shrub. Stem often has black spots. Leaves alternate and egg-shaped; can be 6cm long and 2cm wide.

FLOWERS: Flowers pink or lilac with dark red centre, 5–10cm across with five overlapping rounded lobes. Flowers after good rains at any time of year. Floral emblem of the Northern Territory.

HABITAT/RANGE: Arid dry areas, mainly in central Australia. Found in all mainland states.

Round-leaf Rice-flower *Pimelea nivea*

HEIGHT/ID: 2m. Erect and spreading shrub, branches usually covered with dense white hairs. Leaves flat and oval, partly rounded and grow to 1.5cm; they are dark green and glossy above, nearly white underneath.

FLOWERS: Either white or pale pink, usually in dense terminal heads, 3cm long. Often has slight perfume. Flowers from spring to summer.

HABITAT/RANGE: Widespread in open forest areas of Tasmania.

Qualup Bell *Pimelea physodes*

HEIGHT/ID: 1m. Slender shrub, very erect. Blue-green leaves narrow, oval, flat and 1–3cm long with prominent tip.

FLOWERS: Greenish-yellow and fully enclosed in bracts that form a bell-like pendent. Flower-head up to 6cm long. Flowers from winter to spring.

HABITAT/RANGE: Sandy heathland and forests of Western Australia.

Rose Banjine *Pimelea rosea*

HEIGHT/ID: 1m. Erect, slender shrub. Leaves broad and pointed, 1–2cm long and 6mm across.

FLOWERS: White to rose pink. Terminal heads up to 4cm across. Flowers from winter to summer.

HABITAT/RANGE: Coastal plains of southern Western Australia.

Common Correa *Correa reflexa*

HEIGHT/ID: Up to 2m, but usually 1m. Can be erect shrub or spreading plant. Leaves opposite and pear-shaped.

FLOWERS: Red or cream bell-shaped flowers up to 4cm long with pale (greenish, yellowish or whitish) tips. Up to eight protruding stamens hang from inside flower. Flowers from winter to spring.

HABITAT/RANGE: Found in all states except Western Australia, in a wide variety of habitats.

Forest Boronia *Boronia muelleri*

HEIGHT/ID: 3m. Branches often glandular. Leaves divided and up to 5cm long. Can have many oval, flat leaves which are finely toothed with pointed tips.

FLOWERS: Pale pink flowers with four spreading petals, 2cm across and in clusters of to seven in the axils. Flowers profusely at times. Winter flowering.

HABITAT/RANGE: Mainly coastal areas of Victoria and New South Wales.

Pink Swamp-heath *Sprengelia incarnata*

HEIGHT/ID: 1m. Upright shrub. Leaves up to 2cm long and wrap around the stem.

FLOWERS: Clusters of pink or off-white flowers grow profusely from stem. Flowers from winter to spring.

HABITAT/RANGE: In a variety of soils in New South Wales, Victoria and Tasmania.

Curry Flower *Lysinema ciliatum*

HEIGHT/ID: 70cm. Small slender shrub with egg-shaped leaves up to 6cm long. Leaves can be curry scented.

FLOWERS: White star-shaped flowers up to 2cm long, with brown sepals and dense bracts. Flowers from winter to spring.

HABITAT/RANGE: Sandy soils and gravelly areas of southern Western Australia.

Common Heath *Epacris impressa*

HEIGHT/ID: Up to 2m, usually 1m. Usually tall and erect. Leaves attached to plant stem, often crowded on stem, and are sharply pointed; they can be 15mm long and 6mm wide.

FLOWERS: Stem often crowded with pink or red (sometimes white) bell-shaped flowers on short stalks and arranged in small clusters. Flowers from autumn to spring. The floral emblem of Victoria.

HABITAT/RANGE: Wet or damp areas in heathland or bush in Tasmania, Victoria, eastern New South Wales and south-east South Australia.

Fuchsia Heath *Epacris longiflora*

HEIGHT/ID: 2.2m. Straggling shrub with wiry stalk and hairy branches. The few leaves are bare and almost heart-shaped with rigid spear-like points.

FLOWERS: Red flowers are tubular and up to 3cm long with either brown or white tips. Each petal is singular on stem. Flowers autumn to spring.

HABITAT/RANGE: Flowers almost year-round in coastal areas and tablelands of Victoria, New South Wales and south-east Queensland.

Candle Heath *Richea continentis*

HEIGHT/ID: 1m. Small branched shrub. Stems spread and often take root. Leaves pointed and 2–4cm long with crowded sheath at the base of plant.

FLOWERS: Creamy-white, egg-shaped and nearly 2cm long. Flowers from summer.

HABITAT/RANGE: Alpine and sub-alpine regions of New South Wales and Victoria.

Golden Heath *Styphelia adscendens*

HEIGHT/ID: 40cm. Dense-growing bush with greyish spine-tipped leaves up to 3cm long.

FLOWERS: Yellow to cream tubular flowers at ends of branches; 2–3cm long. The five loose hairy petals appear to roll backwards. Flowers from late winter to spring.

HABITAT/RANGE: Open heathland and bush areas of Victoria, Tasmania and New South Wales.

Flame Heath *Styphelia behrii*

HEIGHT/ID: 40cm. Often in small groups. Leaves flat and pointed.

FLOWERS: Tubular flowers usually red, but can be pink, yellow, cream or green. Flowers from late winter to summer.

HABITAT/RANGE: Heathland and open forest areas of New South Wales, Victoria and South Australia.

Snake-bush *Hemiandra pungens*

HEIGHT/ID: 1m. Usually a spreading plant, but also prostrate in some areas. Leaves fleshy and stiff, usually pointed, mostly flat or concave, up to 12cm long.

FLOWERS: White to mauve-pink, usually with red spots inside. Up to 2cm across with three lobes; upper and lower lips arranged in small auxiliary racemes. Flowers from spring to summer.

HABITAT/RANGE: Sandy heath areas of south-west Western Australia.

Rough Mint-bush *Prostanthera denticulata*

HEIGHT/ID: 1m. Very upright shrub. Leaves opposite, broad, slightly curled and up to 12mm long.

FLOWERS: Usually purple, tubular and up to 12mm long; arranged in pairs on slender leafy stem. Lower lip can be triple-lobed, while upper lip has two lobes. Flowers spring to summer.

HABITAT/RANGE: Gravelly or sandy areas of Victoria and New South Wales.

Fairy Aprons *Utricularia dichotoma*

HEIGHT/ID: 30cm. Erect shrub. An insectivorous herb. Leaves mainly submerged in water, finely divided and modified to trap small insects.

FLOWERS: Usually purple to lilac, sometimes white or yellow. Flowers are terminal, sometimes in small clusters. Flowers from spring to summer.

HABITAT/RANGE: Swamp areas, heathlands and other places with standing water. Found in all states except Northern Territory.

Crimson Turkey Bush *Eremophila latrobei*

HEIGHT/ID: 2m. Erect shrub. Stems warty and covered in fine hairs. Leaves narrow, up to 9cm long and 5cm wide.

FLOWERS: Tubular flowers up to 3cm long, mainly red, covered with fine hairs and with pointed lobes. Stamens extend a few cm beyond end of flower. Flowers from autumn to spring.

HABITAT/RANGE: Widespread in arid areas of all mainland states.

Wild Tomato *Solanum quadriloculatum*

HEIGHT/ID: 50cm. Sprawling shrub. Stems covered in dense hairs and prickles. Leaves egg-shaped and pointed at tip.

FLOWERS: Mainly purple with a yellow centre; 2.5cm across with pointed lobes. Flowers winter to spring.

HABITAT/RANGE: Widespread over much of Australia in a variety of soils. Occurs in all states except Victoria and Tasmania.

Poached Egg Daisy *Polycalymma stuartii*

HEIGHT/ID: 60cm. Erect woolly annual. Pointed grey-green leaves are 2.6cm long and 1.5mm wide, with veins running full length of leaf.

FLOWERS: Heads white with bright yellow centres about 2.5cm across. Flower-head feels papery. One flower per stem. Flowers from spring to summer or when rain falls.

HABITAT/RANGE: Sandy areas in dry, arid regions of Outback Australia.

Snow Daisy *Celmisia longifolia*

HEIGHT/ID: 30cm. Erect perennial. Very hairy silver leaves are linear or pear-shaped; they grow from base of plant, have curled-under margins and can be 25cm long.

FLOWERS: White with yellow centre, up to 2.5cm across. One flower per stem. Flowers from summer to autumn.

HABITAT/RANGE: Widespread in snow and high country of Tasmania, Victoria and New South Wales.

Fleshy Groundsel *Senecio gregorii*

HEIGHT/ID: 40cm. Very erect herb. Bluish-green leaves are thick, fleshy and pointed, growing to 2.9cm long.

FLOWERS: Brilliant bright yellow daisy-like flower. Solitary flower-head per stem. Flower-head about 5cm across with 8–12 florets. Flowers at any time, depending on rainfall.

HABITAT/RANGE: Widespread in arid mallee country of mainland Australia.

Minnie Daisy *Minuria leptophylla*

HEIGHT/ID: 50cm. Multi-branched. Narrow leaves up to 4cm long and 1cm wide; becoming smaller towards top.

FLOWERS: Petals vary from lilac to pink-purple, usually with a yellow centre. Can sometimes have up to 30 florets or petals.

HABITAT/RANGE: Widely distributed over much of Australia. In all states except Tasmania.

Pink Everlasting *Schoenia cassiniana*

HEIGHT/ID: 50cm. Small herb. Leaves sword-shaped, up to 7cm long and very densely covered with fine hairs. Some short leaves may occur on stem.

FLOWERS: Pink papery bract flowers with yellow centres in a terminal cluster. Each flower has about 10 tubular petals. Flowers in spring.

HABITAT/RANGE: Arid and semi-arid regions of South Australia, Western Australia and Northern Territory.

Spiked Dampiera   *Dampiera spicigera*

HEIGHT/ID: 30cm. Erect perennial herb with many branches, usually grey or yellow and covered with hairs. Leaves oblong, toothed and up to 4cm long.

FLOWERS: Masses of blue flowers on leafless stems cover the entire plant. Flowers in spring.

HABITAT/RANGE: Heavy soils in south-west Western Australia.

Blue Leschenaultia *Lechenaultia biloba*

HEIGHT/ID: 80cm. Low and straggling shrub. Leaves needle-like and crowded, up to 1.5cm long; they are soft and feel partly fleshy.

FLOWERS: Delicate tubular flowers in various shades of blue. Up to 2cm long with five wedge-shaped lobes and hairy insides. Flowers from late winter to spring.

HABITAT/RANGE: Gravel areas of south-west Western Australia.

Red Leschenaultia *Lechenaultia formosa*

HEIGHT/ID: 50cm. Mainly prostrate shrub, stems may be spreading or partly erect. Fleshy leaves are linear, pointed, usually crowded and up to 1cm long.

FLOWERS: Colour variable but mainly in red. Flower 2–4mm across. Flowers from winter to spring.

HABITAT/RANGE: Southern coasts and hinterlands in Western Australia.

Fairy Fan-flower *Scaevola aemula*

HEIGHT/ID: 50cm. Sprawling perennial herb with ascending stems covered in yellow hairs. Leaves egg-shaped and slightly toothed, 2cm long and 4mm wide.

FLOWERS: From lilac to pink and spreading to one side like a fan, the terminal spikes are 24cm long. Flowers from spring to autumn.

HABITAT/RANGE: Coastal areas of New South Wales, Victoria, Queensland and South Australia.

Crab Claws *Stylidium macranthum*

HEIGHT/ID: 30cm. Erect shrub. Leaves are smooth and pointed, up to 30cm long.

FLOWERS: Flowers usually pink and resemble a crab's claw. Up to 2.5cm long.

HABITAT/RANGE: Sandy heaths and swamp areas in the Esperance area of Western Australia.

Grass Trigger-plant *Stylidium graminifolium*

HEIGHT/ID: 70cm. Upright perennial with long flowering stems. Leaves linear with curved margins and pointed tips; sometimes they are finely toothed, as well tufted at the base of the plant.

FLOWERS: Four spreading petals can be pink or magenta with a white centre. Unusual because has two stamens united in a long bent column, and when touched they spring closed. Spring and summer flowering.

HABITAT/RANGE: Dry forest areas, coastal regions and inland slopes in New South Wales, Queensland and Victoria.

GLOSSARY

Acute: having a sharp point.

Alternate: leaves on a stem, arranged at different levels, or not opposite each other.

Anther: pollen-bearing part of a stamen.

Axis: main part of a stem of a plant.

Bract: modified leaf structure that lacks a blade.

Calli: glands on labella of orchid which do not secrete.

Erect: plants that grow upright.

Floret: a small flower.

Foliage: the leaves of a plant.

Glabrous: smooth and without hairs.

Glandular: bearing glands or glandular hairs.

Habitat: the area or environment where plant grows.

Herbaceous: perennial plant that dies down after each flowering period.

Herb: plant used for medicine, food or scent.

Labellum: front petal of orchid.

Lanceolate: shaped like a lance and tapering at both ends.

Linear: long and narrow with both sides parallel.

Lobe: rounded part of leaf or petal.

Nectar: sweet fluid secreted from plant.

Oblong: leaf which is broader than it is long, with both ends rounded.

Obovate: egg-shaped with the broadest area in or above the middle.

Pendulous: hanging downwards.

Perennial: a plant that lives for more than two seasons.

Perfume: sweet scent, or a fragrant substance which emits an agreeable scent.

Petiole: the stalk of a leaf.

Phyllode: flat leaf or stalk.

Pinnate: leaves divided and arranged on each side of stalk, usually opposite each other.

Prostrate: plants that grow flat by creeping along the ground.

Pubescent: plants that are covered with short, soft or downy hairs

Pungent: leaves or plants that have a strong smell.

Recurved: leaves that curl downwards or backwards.

Raceme: unbranched cluster of flowers along a stem.

Rosette: leaves radiating in a circle from a central point.

Sac: a shallow pouch or cavity.

Sepal: leaf-like segment of the calyx.

Serrated: with sharp forward points.

Shoot: new growth from plant.

Spreading: plants that extend foliage.

Stamen: the male pollen-bearing organ of a flowering plant.

Style: long structure connecting stigma to ovary.

Succulent: with soft juicy flesh.

Sucker: new shoots appearing from main plant.

Terminal: situated at the end or top.

Terrestrial: growing in the ground.

Tuber: most orchids have a tuber or thickened roots.

Undulate: giving the appearance of waves.

Vein: structural tissues of a leaf, used to move water and minerals.

Viscous: sticky area of plant.

Winged: parts of the plant that are arranged on an axis.

INDEX

A

Acacia brachybotrya 128
Acacia cardiophylla 125
Acacia gladiiformis 128
Acacia glaucoptera 127
Acacia kempeana 126
Acacia longifolia 125
Acacia podalyriifolia 127
Acacia spectabilis 124
Adenanthos barbiger 99
Albany Synaphea 64
Alpine Greenhood 16
Alyogyne huegelii 160
Anigozanthos humilis 61
Anigozanthos manglesii 59
Anigozanthos rufus 62
Anigozanthos viridis 60
Anzybas unguiculatus 39

B

Banded Bee Orchid 43
Banded Tree Spider
 Orchid 48
Banksia baueri 73
Banksia caleyi 75
Banksia coccinea 71
Banksia falcata 80
Banksia formosa 78
Banksia gardneri 69
Banksia laevigata 72
Banksia marginata 70
Banksia nobilis 77

Banksia ornata 75
Banksia polycephala 79
Banksia repens 76
Banksia sessilis 77
Banksia spinulosa 74
Banksia undata 79
Batchelor's Buttons 107
Bauera sessiliflora 109
Baxter's Kunzea 149
Bearded Greenhood 22
Beaufortia heterophylla 151
Beaufortia orbifolia 151
Beaufortia schaueri 150
Beaufortia sparsa 152
Beaufortia squarrosa 152
Black Bluebush 106
Black Gin 58
Black Kangaroo Paw 63
Blandfordia nobilis 10
Blotched Cane Orchid 17
Blotched Sun Orchid 55
Blue Leschenaultia 181
Blue Tinsel-lily 58
Blunt Greenhood 15
Bonnet Orchid 49
Boorman's Rustyhood 21
Boronia muelleri 165
Bracelet Honey-myrtle 135
Brachysema celsianum 122
Broombush 142
Bunochilus macilentus 15

C

Caladenia bryceana ssp.
 bryceana 31
Caladenia clavigera 29
Caladenia filamentosa 28
Caladenia latifolia 28
Caladenia longicauda 30
Caleana major 32
Calectasia cyanea 58
Callistemon brachyandrus
 156
Callistemon pachyphyllus
 155
Callistemon pallidus 153
Callistemon rigidus 155
Callistemon rugulosus 154
Callistemon subulatus 156
Calochilus robertsonii 41
Calytrix exstipulata 158
Candle Heath 169
Cauliflower Hakea 94
Celmisia longifolia 177
Cepobaculum semifuscum
 47
Ceratobium dalbertisii 52
Chamelaucium uncinatum
 157
Chenille Honey-myrtle 137
Chittick 100
Christmas Bells 10
Clubbed Spider Orchid 29
Coastal Hakea 92

Cockies' Tongues 114
Comb Grevillea 88
Comb-leaf Grevillea 84
Common Cat's Paw 61
Common Correa 164
Common Elbow Orchid 39
Common Flat-pea 120
Common Golden Moths 37
Common Heath 167
Common Popflower 104
Common Potato Orchid 44
Common Smokebush 101
Common Wedge-pea 118
Conospermum stoechadis 101
Cooktown Orchid 54
Corky Honey-myrtle 138
Correa reflexa 164
Corysanthes diemenica 40
Crab Claws 184
Creeping Banksia 76
Crimson Turkey Bush 174
Crotalaria cunninghamii 112
Cryptostylis erecta 49
Cryptostylis subulata 31
Curry Flower 166
Cut-leaf Guinea Flower 102
Cyanicula amplexans 36
Cymbidium madidum 12
Cymbidium suave 13

D

Daddy Long-legs Orchid 28
Dainty Blue China Orchid 36
Dampiera spicigera 180
Darwinia oldfieldii 157

Daviesia leptophylla 119
Dendrobium speciosum 33
Desert Banksia 75
Dillwynia sericea 121
Diplodium coccinum 18
Diplodium tenuissimum 19
Dipodium punctatum 32
Diuris chryseopsis 37
Diuris daltonii 38
Diuris laxiflora 43
Dockrillia racemosa 45
Dockrillia striolata 46
Drosera auriculata 108
Dwarf Bottlebrush 156
Dwarf Jester Orchid 31
Dwarf Wedge-pea 117

E

Elythranthera brunonis 35
Elythranthera emarginata 35
Enfield Grevillea 90
Epacris impressa 167
Epacris longiflora 168
Erect Pencil Orchid 45
Eremophila latrobei 174
Eriochilus cucullatus 56

F

Fairy Aprons 173
Fairy Bells 51
Fairy Fan-flower 183
Fire Bush 123
Flame Grevillea 83
Flame Heath 170
Flat Wattle 127
Fleshy Groundsel 178

Flying Duck Orchid 32
Forest Boronia 165
Fragrant Tea-tree Orchid 47
Fuchsia Grevillea 80
Fuchsia Heath 168

G

Gastrodia sesamoides 44
Geraldton Wax 157
Giant Boat-lip Orchid 12
Glischrocaryon aureum 104
Glossodia major 53
Golden Dryandra 77
Golden Heath 169
Gompholobium ecostatum 117
Gompholobium huegelii 118
Gomphrena canescens 107
Gossypium sturtianum 161
Graceful Honey-myrtle 145
Grampians Bauera 109
Grampians Leafy Greenhood 15
Granite Honey-myrtle 144
Grass Trigger-plant 185
Grass-leaved Hakea 98
Grassy Boat-lip Orchid 13
Great Sun Orchid 27
Green Antelope Orchid 52
Green Bird Orchid 38
Green Birdflower 112
Green Kangaroo Paw 60
Green-flowered Paperbark 147
Grevillea alpina 85
Grevillea aquifolium 87

INDEX

Grevillea banksii 81
Grevillea bedggoodiana 90
Grevillea bipinnatifida 80
Grevillea eriostachya 83
Grevillea huegelii 88
Grevillea lanigera 82
Grevillea leucopteris 89
Grevillea longistyla 91
Grevillea parallela 86
Grevillea pectinata 84
Grevillea petrophiloides 81
Grevillea pinaster 90
Grevillea sp. 90
Grevillea wickhamii 91
Grey Mulga 128

H

Hairpin Banksia 74
Hairy Jugflower 99
Hakea bucculenta 94
Hakea clavata 92
Hakea corymbosa 94
Hakea cristata 96
Hakea cucullata 97
Hakea laurina 93
Hakea multilineata 98
Hakea petiolaris 95
Hemiandra pungens 171
Hibbertia cuneiformis 102
Hibbertia procumbens 103
Hibiscus panduriformis 160
Holly Grevillea 87
Hyacinth Orchid 32

I

Isopogon anethifolius 66

Isopogon latifolius 67
Isopogon sp. 67

J

Jug Orchid 20

K

Kennedia prostrata 113
King Hakea 97
King Orchid 33
Kingia australis 58
Kunzea ambigua 150
Kunzea baxteri 149
Kunzea parvifolia 148

L

Lambertia formosa 65
Lambertia inermis 100
Large Boulder Orchid 52
Large Spider Orchid 30
Leafless Parson's Bands 56
Lechenaultia biloba 181
Lechenaultia formosa 182
Lemon Bottlebrush 153
Leptosema chambersii 111
Leptospermum nitidum 159
Lilac Hibiscus 160
Long-leaved Petrophile 98
Long-style Grevillea 91
Lyperanthus serratus 42
Lysinema ciliatum 166

M

Macropidia fuliginosa 63
Maireana pyramidata 106
Many-headed Dryandra 79
Matted Bush-pea 116

Melaleuca armillaris 135
Melaleuca decussata 139
Melaleuca elliptica 144
Melaleuca ericifolia 134
Melaleuca filifolia 140
Melaleuca fulgens 139
Melaleuca huegelii 137
Melaleuca lateritia 146
Melaleuca nesophila 145
Melaleuca nodosa 141
Melaleuca pentagona 143
Melaleuca radula 145
Melaleuca scabra 144
Melaleuca sp. 136, 143
Melaleuca styphelioides 141
Melaleuca suberosa 138
Melaleuca thymoides 138
Melaleuca uncinata 142
Melaleuca viridiflora 147
Melaleuca wilsonii 140
Minnie Daisy 179
Minuria leptophylla 179
Monga Waratah 67
Mountain Devil 65
Mountain Grevillea 85
Mudgee Wattle 124

N

Narrow-leaf Bitter-pea 119
Narrow-leaved Drumsticks 66
Nodding Blue Lily 57
Nodding Greenhood 16

O

Oldfield's Darwinia 157
Oligochaetochilus boormanii 21

P

Painted Featherflower 129
Parrot Bush 77
Patersonia occidentalis 11
Petalochilus carneus 34
Petrophile longifolia 98
Pimelea nivea 162
Pimelea physodes 163
Pimelea rosea 163
Pincushion Hakea 93
Pink Bottlebrush 150
Pink Enamel Orchid 35
Pink Everlasting 179
Pink Fairy Orchid 28
Pink Fingers 34
Pink Mulla Mulla 105
Pink Pokers 81
Pink Spiral Orchid 50
Pink Swamp-heath 166
Pink-bells 110
Platylobium obtusangulum 120
Plumatichilos plumosum 22
Poached Egg Daisy 176
Polycalymma stuartii 176
Prasophyllum odoratum 36
Prickly Bottlebrush 156
Prickly Dryandra 80
Prickly Paperbark 141
Prickly-leaved Paperbark 141

Prostanthera denticulata 172
Prostrate Banksia 69
Pterostylis alpina 16
Pterostylis curta 15
Pterostylis nutans 16
Ptilotus exaltatus 105
Pultenaea pedunculata 116
Purple Beard Orchid 41
Purple Enamel Orchid 35
Purple Flags 11
Pyrorchis nigricans 14

Q

Qualup Bell 163
Queen of Sheba 26
Queensland Silver Wattle 127

R

Rattle Beaks 42
Ravensthorpe Bottlebrush 151
Red Beaks Orchid 14
Red Kangaroo Paw 62
Red Lantern Banksia 75
Red Leschenaultia 182
Red Pokers Hakea 94
Red-and-green Kangaroo Paw 59
Richea continentis 169
Robin Red-breast Bush 146
Roe's Featherflower 131
Rose Banjine 163
Rough Honey-myrtle 144
Rough Mint-bush 172

Round-leaf Rice-flower 162
Running Postman 113

S

Salmon Sun Orchid 25
Sand Bottlebrush 152
Sarcochilus ceciliae 51
Sarcochilus hartmannii 52
Scaevola aemula 183
Scarlet Banksia 71
Scarlet Bottlebrush 154
Scarlet Greenhood 18
Scarlet Honey-myrtle 139
Scented Leek Orchid 36
Schoenia cassiniana 179
Sea Urchin Hakea 95
Senecio gregorii 178
Senna pleurocarpa 123
Shiny Tea-tree 159
Showy Dryandra 78
Showy Honey-myrtle 145
Showy Parrot-pea 121
Silky Oak Grevillea 81
Silver Banksia 70
Silver Grevillea 86
Simpliglottis cornuta 38
Slender Sun Orchid 23
Small Helmet Orchid 39
Snail Hakea 96
Snake-bush 171
Snow Daisy 177
Solanum quadriloculatum 175
Spiked Dampiera 180
Spiranthes australis 50
Spotted Sun Orchid 24

INDEX

Spreading Guinea Flower 103
Sprengelia incarnata 166
Stamnorchis recurva 20
Stately Helmet Orchid 40
Stiff Bottlebrush 155
Stirling Range Bottlebrush 151
Streaked Rock Orchid 46
Sturt's Desert Pea 115
Sturt's Desert Rose 161
Stylidium graminifolium 185
Stylidium macranthum 184
Stypandra glauca 57
Styphelia adscendens 169
Styphelia behrii 170
Swainsona formosa 115
Swamp Bottlebrush 152
Swamp Greenhood 19
Swamp Paperbark 134
Swan River Pea 122
Sword-leaf Wattle 128
Sydney Golden Wattle 125
Synaphea polymorpha 64

T

Tall Sundew 108
Telopea mongaensis 67
Telopea speciosissima 68
Templetonia retusa 114
Tennis Ball Banksia 72
Tetrabaculum tetragonum 48
Tetratheca ciliata 110
Thelychiton graciliacaulis 17
Thelymitra aristata 27
Thelymitra benthamiana 55
Thelymitra ixioides 24
Thelymitra pauciflora 23
Thelymitra rubra 25
Thelymitra speciosa 26
Thynninorchis huntianus 39
Tick Bush 150
Tongue Orchid 31
Totem Poles 139
Turkey Bush 158

U

Upside-down Plant 111
Urchin Dryandra 79
Utricularia dichotoma 173

V

Vappodes phalaenopsis 54
Verticordia chrysantha 130
Verticordia etheliana 132
Verticordia monadelpha 130
Verticordia oculata 133
Verticordia picta 129
Verticordia roei 131
Verticordia sp. 132, 133
Violet Kunzea 148

W

Wallum Bottlebrush 155
Waratah 68
Wax-lip Orchid 53
West Wyalong Wattle 125
Western Purple Donkey Orchid 38
White-plumed Grevillea 89
Wickham's Grevillea 91
Wild Tomato 175
Wilson's Honey-myrtle 140
Wiry Honey-myrtle 140
Witchetty Bush 126
Woolly Banksia 73
Woolly Featherflower 130
Woolly Grevillea 82

Y

Yellow Featherflower 130
Yellow Hibiscus 160

OTHER TITLES IN THE SERIES

Gu

Bristo

Pub Walks

Nigel Vile

The Kennet and Avon Canal near Freshford

COUNTRYSIDE BOOKS
NEWBURY BERKSHIRE

First published 2017
© Nigel Vile 2017

COUNTRYSIDE BOOKS
3 Catherine Road
Newbury, Berkshire

To view our complete range of books,
please visit us at
www.countrysidebooks.co.uk

ISBN 978 1 84674 348 1

Photographs by Nigel Vile
Cover design by Barrie Appleby

Designed by KT Designs, St Helens
Produced through The Letterworks Ltd., Reading
Typeset by KT Designs, St Helens
Printed in Poland

Introduction

What better way to spend a leisurely few hours than to stretch your legs and then visit a traditional pub for well-earned drink or bite to eat? The 20 walks in this book allow you to do just that. Each route – that includes, or is just a short drive from, a recommended pub – takes you through some of the finest scenery in the Bristol and Bath area.

The variety of landscape in this part of the country is both rich and diverse. To the west is the Severn Estuary and the Bristol Channel with far-ranging and expansive views, and where the extensive mud flats at low tide make for an ornithologist's paradise. Inland lie the Cotswold Hills, where the honey-coloured cottages and picture-postcard villages maintain their endless appeal. To the south the limestone creates the rugged landscape of the Mendip Hills. Here are some of the more strenuous walks in the region, with the hilltops nudging that seemingly magical 1,000 ft contour line.

A sketch map indicating the route to be followed accompanies each walk. However, I would always recommend carrying the relevant OS Explorer map as well. The appropriate sheet number is given at the start of each walk.

To make your day complete, do not forget to carry a snack and a drink in that trusty rucksack, as well as a decent set of waterproofs – despite occasional belief to the contrary, authors of walking guidebooks cannot guarantee their readers sunny weather!

Nigel Vile

Publisher's Note

We hope that you obtain considerable enjoyment from this book: great care has been taken in its preparation. However, changes of landlord and actual pub closures are sadly not uncommon. Likewise, although at the time of publication all routes followed public rights of way or permitted paths, diversion orders can be made and permissions withdrawn.

We cannot, of course, be responsible for such diversion orders and any inaccuracies in the text which result from these or any other changes to the routes, nor any damage which might result from walkers trespassing

Guide to Bristol & Bath Pub Walks

on private property. We are anxious though that all details covering the walks and the pubs are kept up to date and would therefore welcome information from readers which would be relevant to future editions.

The Inn, Freshford

Oldbury Pill

1 Littleton upon Severn

6½ miles (10.4km)

WALK HIGHLIGHTS

Over 2 miles of the coastal path alongside the Severn Estuary between Littleton and Oldbury are followed on this walk, as well as the countryside that borders the two villages. The estuary supports many wading birds, 100,000 in a typical winter. One particular highlight is the magnificent church dedicated to St Arilda at Oldbury. There is also Whale Wharf, a one-time diminutive port that exported local bricks and imported Welsh coal, where in 1885 a whale became stranded on the outgoing tide, attracting huge interest from the local populace.

THE PUB

The White Hart www.whitehartbristol.com
☎ 01454 412275 **BS35 1NR**

THE WALK

Facing the White Hart, follow the road to the right passing the local Evangelical church and the village hall to reach a junction with Field Lane, 350 yards on from the village hall. Turn left into Field Lane. In 200 yards, there are stiles and footpaths on either side of the road. At this point, cross the stile on the right and walk up the right edge of the field ahead. In the top right corner of the field, cross a stile behind some bushes, walk ahead for a few paces and cross a stile on the left. Walk

5

HOW TO GET THERE AND PARKING: Leave the M48 at Junction 1 by the First Severn Crossing and follow the B4461 towards Alveston and Thornbury. In 2 miles, in the village of Elberton, turn left onto an unclassified road signposted to Littleton upon Severn. The White Hart is on the right in 1¼ miles, just beyond a right-hand bend by the local village hall. Either park on the roadside in front of the village hall or there is a car park behind the pub for patrons. **Postcode** BS35 1NR

MAP: OS Explorer 167 Thornbury, Dursley & Yate. **Grid ref** 596901.

across the field ahead to a stile in its bottom right corner, walk ahead to a junction with a path and turn left to a handgate. Follow a gravelled track uphill to a gate and hilltop field, continue ahead on this track to a gate on the far side of the field. Cross one final field, bearing right all the while, to a gate and track shown as Bond Lane on the OS map.

2 Follow this track to the left to its junction with a road in ½ mile just past a property. Turn left and, in 300 yards, turn right onto a track shown as Stock Lane on the OS map. In ½ mile, at a junction with a road, cross over and follow the bridleway opposite. Keep left at a junction in 500 yards and continue for 300 yards to a road on the edge of Oldbury-on-Severn. Turn left and walk along to the church, walk around the right edge of the church enjoying views of the Severn, before dropping downhill on the far side of the churchyard to a gate. Beyond this gate, turn right to a gate in the hedge on the right and walk across the field ahead to a stile in the opposite field boundary. Walk down the left edge of the next field to a stile and a lane by Westmarsh House. Turn right and follow the lane for 350 yards to the 'main road' in Oldbury-on-Severn.

3 Turn left and, in a few paces, follow a footpath on the left – the Severn Way – through a complex of horse stables to reach a flood defence and the Severn in ¼ mile. Follow this flood defence, a raised grassy embankment, to the left for 1¼ miles to an inlet known as Whale Wharf. Pass through a handgate and continue following the Severn downstream for ¼ mile to a footpath marker sign on the left. Drop down to a gate and enter an open field. Walk across the field ahead to a stile in its opposite boundary before crossing a second field to a gate and stile. Beyond this

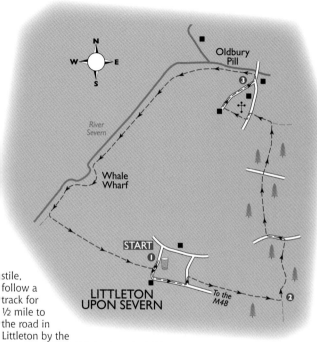

stile,
follow a
track for
½ mile to
the road in
Littleton by the
village hall. Turn left back to the White Hart.

PLACES OF INTEREST NEARBY

The nearby village of Aust is worth visiting to explore the decaying
remains of the old **Severn Ferry Terminal**, as well as **Aust Cliff**, a fossil
hunter's paradise. (www.ukfossils.co.uk/2010/03/04/aust-cliff)

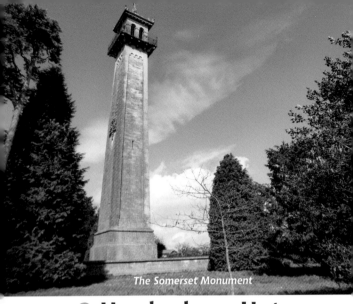
The Somerset Monument

2 **Hawkesbury Upton**
5 miles (8 km)

WALK HIGHLIGHTS
The Cotswold Escarpment, known colloquially as 'The Edge', is where the high open ground of the Cotswold Plateau drops steeply away to the Severn Vale. It is this landscape that is explored on this walk. Enjoy the picturesque Kilcott Valley, where stone cottages and sparkling streams, sheep pasture and wooded hillsides present an idyllic Cotswold feel. Also on the route is the Somerset Monument, erected in 1846 to commemorate the soldier son of the 5th Duke of Beaufort, who served with distinction at Waterloo.

THE PUB
The Beaufort Arms www.beaufortarms.com
☎ 01454 238217 **GL9 1AU**

HOW TO GET THERE AND PARKING: Leave the A46 at Dunkirk, between Bath and Stroud, to follow an unclassified road signposted to Hawkesbury Upton. In 1½ miles, the Beaufort Arms is on the High Street on the left-hand side. Just past the pub is the village hall with its adjoining car-park. A voluntary donation is welcome, the money going towards the upkeep of this vital village amenity. **Postcode** GL9 1AU

MAP: OS Explorer 167 Thornbury, Dursley & Yate **Grid Ref** 777870.

THE WALK

Leave the car park, turn left, walking past the Beaufort Arms, to a junction at the end of Hawkesbury Upton's High Street just past the Fox Inn. Turn left along the road signposted to Starveall, keeping left at an

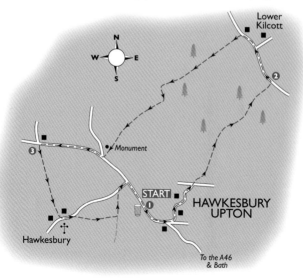

early junction into Back Street. Follow this road as its winds its way out of the village to reach a road junction in 350 yards. Follow the footpath opposite that bears right down to a handgate and field. Continue across the field ahead, dropping downhill through three fields into a valley. In a fourth field, continue to a small footbridge over a stream before following a track to the right down to gate and wooded combe. Follow the grassy path through the bottom of this combe, ignoring occasional tracks that climb the adjoining hillsides, to reach a gate and the lane in the Kilcott valley in ½ mile.

2 Turn left and follow the lane for 600 yards to reach Mickley Cottage on the right. At this point, turn left and follow the Cotswold Way uphill, keeping left at a fork in 300 yards. Pass through a gateway at the top of a climb in 150 yards before bearing right into a hilltop field. Walk along the left edge of this field before entering Claypit Wood at the end of the field. Follow the path through this woodland for 250 yards before passing through a gateway on the left to follow a path up the left edge of a field. At the top of this field, turn right and follow the path for ½ mile to the road immediately past the Somerset Monument. Turn right and, shortly, turn left at a junction to follow a quiet lane downhill signposted to Wickwar.

3 In 600 yards, at a junction by a cottage, pass through a gateway on the left and follow what was once a road – it is now a track – for ½ mile to the road in Hawkesbury by a property called the Carpenter's Shop. Follow the road to the left, passing the church and a neighbouring property, before veering right to follow a path to shortly enter woodland. Follow the path ahead uphill through the woodland to a gate and stile and field. Bear left across the field ahead to a stile in the far left corner of the field. Beyond this stile, walk up the left edges of two fields to join the Cotswold Way, before turning left to join a road in 200 yards. Turn right along to the main road in Hawkesbury Upton by the Drovers' Pool. Follow the main road to the right back to the village hall and its car park.

PLACES OF INTEREST NEARBY

Westonbirt Arboretum (www.forestry.gov.uk/westonbirt). This amazing woodland has 15,000 tree specimens from across the globe, and is well worth a visit.

3 **Old Sodbury**

5½ miles (8.9 km)

WALK HIGHLIGHTS

This walk explores an extensive stretch of the 'The Edge', where you'll find hillforts at Horton and Old Sodbury with commanding views. Various landmarks to look for include the Black Mountains, the Severn Bridges, the Mendip Hills and the Severn Vale.

THE PUB

The Dog Inn www.the-dog-inn.co.uk
☎ 01454 312006   BS37 6LZ

THE WALK

Walk back to the A432 and cross into Cotswold Lane. Almost immediately, veer left and walk down to a farmyard and on to a gate before crossing the field ahead to a gate in its far right corner. Walk across bottom of the next field, with Old Sodbury church on right, to reach a handgate in the end field boundary. Continue following the path across right edges of four fields to reach a lane, cross to a gate opposite and walk across to

Guide to Bristol & Bath Pub Walks

HOW TO GET THERE AND PARKING: Leave the A46 by Cross Hands Hotel, two miles north of Junction 18 for Bath on the M4 motorway, and follow the A432 for one mile into Old Sodbury. The Dog Inn is on the left-hand side before a crossroads in the village centre. Immediately past the pub, turn left into Chapel Lane and park roadside. **Postcode** BS37 6LZ

MAP: OS Explorer 167 Thornbury, Dursley & Yate. **Grid Ref** 753815.

far right corner of the field ahead to join road in Little Sodbury. Turn left and walk along to a junction immediately past the village church, before turning right on road signposted to Horton and A46.

2 In 100 yards, by end of some cottages, turn left along a path that runs alongside the last cottage to a stile. Turn left – Cotswold Way – and walk along bottom left edges of two fields. Drop downhill in third field, fishing lake on right, before climbing steeply uphill to a gate. Continue along enclosed path between horse paddocks to reach a gate before keeping ahead to join main road in Horton. Turn right before taking first left by the village school. Immediately past the school, turn right up to a gate and hillside field. Walk up the right edge of this field to a handgate on right just behind school, pass through this gateway and follow footpath ahead as it climbs uphill to reach a folly. Continue past the folly to footpath sign and gate on left on the hilltop. Pass through gateway, walk ahead to the ramparts of Horton Fort, turn right, climb over ramparts and walk across to a gate, National Trust sign and lane in corner of the field.

3 Follow lane to the right to a junction in 350 yards. Follow road to the right that heads down into Horton and, in 50 yards, on a bend, turn left and follow a quiet lane across hilltop for ½ mile to a road junction. Cross road to a gap in the wall opposite and follow path across field ahead to its far right corner. Beyond a handgate, walk across right edge of a lawn to reach a parking area by barn conversions. Pass through gate in far right corner of parking area, turn left and follow a path alongside a barn conversion to a gate on left. Beyond gate, walk ahead for 25 yards before turning right through the ramparts of Sodbury Fort.

Cross to ramparts opposite before keeping ahead to a gate. Turn right and follow a path that drops down the Cotswold escarpment. In 150 yards, at bottom of the hill, pass through gateway on left and follow a path – Cotswold Way – across top left edge of a hillside field with views. Pass through gate at end of the field, cross a small field to another gate and follow path down to the road by Old Sodbury school. Turn right and walk along to, and through, the churchyard by Old Sodbury church. Pass through a gate at the end of the churchyard, drop downhill to a gate in bottom left corner of the field ahead before crossing the next field to reach a farmyard. Walk through this and back to A432 and the pub.

PLACES OF INTEREST NEARBY

The attractive market town of **Chipping Sodbury,** whose wide main street is the site of a bi-annual **Mop Fair**, is a small town dominated by delightful independent retailers.

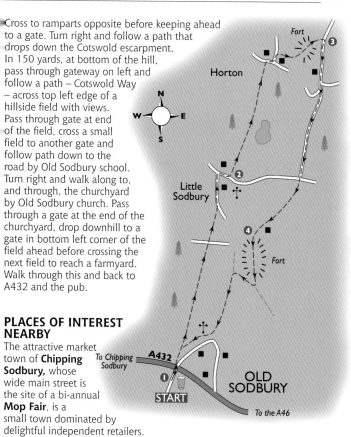

View across Doynton

4 Doynton
5½ miles (8.9 km)

WALK HIGHLIGHTS
This walk from Doynton follows the River Boyd and a section of the Monarch's Way, the escape route taken by King Charles II in 1651 after being defeated at the Battle of Worcester. In Dyrham, the walk passes the 'back door' to Dyrham House, with a tantalising glimpse of the beautiful gardens created by William Blathwayt. Also expect views of the Severn Vale, the Mendip Hills, much of Bristol's urban landscape and the more distant Welsh hills.

THE PUB
The Cross House Inn www.thecrosshousedoynton.com
☎ 0117 329 5830 **BS30 5TF**

THE WALK
1 Head up Bury Lane then Church Road to the church. Walk through the churchyard to a gate in the end boundary wall. Cross the field ahead to a gate before bearing half-right in the following field to a gate in the

HOW TO GET THERE AND PARKING: Leave the A46 at Cold Ashton north of Bath, and follow the A420 towards Bristol. In 3 miles, in the village of Wick, turn right and follow the road signposted to Doynton. The Cross House Inn lies in the centre of the village, where there is roadside parking. **Postcode** BS30 5TF

MAP: OS Explorer 155 Bristol & Bath. **Grid ref** 719740.

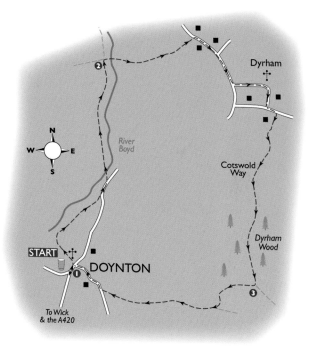

right-hand field boundary. Follow the left edges of the next 2 fields to a footbridge over a stream at the end of the second field, before bearing right in the following field to a stile in the hedgerow and Doynton Lane. Turn left and follow the lane for 250 yards to a gate and bridleway on the left, ignoring an earlier footpath. Cross the River Boyd just beyond this gate, turn right and follow the right edges of 5 fields to a pair of handgates at the end of the fifth field.

2 Enter the next field and, in 25 yards, cross a footbridge on the right and walk across the right edges of 3 fields, passing through gateways along the way. In a fourth field, bear left across to a gate in the left-hand field boundary by a telegraph pole. Join a road, turn right and walk past Talbot Farm and continue for ¼ mile to a junction on the edge of Dyrham. Turn left and follow a road around past the rear of Dyrham House and onto a junction at the top of Dyrham's main street. Turn left and, in 100 yards, just past the Old Post Office Cottage, turn right onto the Cotswold Way. Follow what is an enclosed path for 600 yards to a pond, before following the Cotswold Way ahead across 4 fields, climbing uphill in the fourth field to reach a gate at the entrance to Dyrham Wood. Follow the path uphill through the woodland to reach a field in 300 yards.

3 Do not follow the Cotswold Way ahead at this point; instead, turn right and follow a permissive path that winds its way around the edge of Dyrham Wood to reach a marker post in the bottom corner of the field. Turn left and walk across the bottom of the field to a gate, before crossing the next field to reach a fence on the right and a stile, a fine view below to Doynton and beyond. Walk down the right edges of 5 fields to a handgate in the right-hand boundary in the bottom corner of the fifth field. Join a grassy track and turn left. In a few paces, where this track bears left, pass through the gateway ahead and follow the right edge of the field ahead to a gap at the bottom of the field. Walk across to a gate in the far corner of the next field and a lane in Doynton. Turn right and walk down to a junction by the church from where it's a short distance back to the Cross House Inn.

PLACES OF INTEREST NEARBY
Dyrham House and Park (www.nationaltrust.org.uk/dyrham-park).

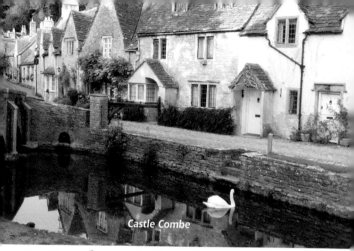

Castle Combe

5 Ford and Castle Combe

4½ miles (7.2 km)

WALK HIGHLIGHTS

The walk starts in the Wiltshire village of Ford, where an 'Old Coach Road' hints at the origins of the settlement. This was a stopping off point on the coach road from London to Bristol, with the White Hart being a centuries-old coaching inn whose garden borders the clear waters of the By Brook. The river valley is followed through to Castle Combe. This picturesque village, with its stone cottages, market cross and ancient bridge, has featured in many films, including the 1967 version of _Doctor Dolittle_ and the 2010 film _War Horse_.

THE PUB

The White Hart www.whitehart-ford.com
☎ 01249 782213 **SN14 8RP**

THE WALK

Return to the A420 and follow the pavement opposite to the right. In 200 yards, just past By Brook Barn, turn left and follow a quiet lane

Guide to Bristol & Bath Pub Walks

HOW TO GET THERE AND PARKING: Ford lies on the A420 between Bristol and Chippenham, 5 miles from Chippenham itself. In the village, take the unclassified road signposted to Colerne and the White Hart is on the left-hand side in 100 yards. The pub has a large parking area. If you are not using the pub, there is a layby on the A420 opposite the now redundant church. **Postcode** SN14 8RP

MAP: OS Explorer 156 Chippenham & Bradford-on-Avon **Grid Ref** 841748.

uphill for 200 yards to a stile on the right. Walk across the field ahead to a stile opposite, turn right and follow an enclosed path to a gate before dropping downhill for 200 yards to a gate on the left, just before the By Brook and Long Dean. Beyond this gate, walk ahead to a wooden footbridge before keeping ahead across a field with the By Brook on the right-hand side. Keep walking ahead through the valley to reach a property in ¼ mile, crossing a footbridge along the way. Just past this property, cross a bridge over the By Brook and turn left to walk along towards a fence.

❷ Just before the fence, bear right and follow a path uphill to its junction with a track in 150 yards. Turn left and follow what is a well-defined track for ¼ mile to a marker post and a faint junction of paths. Veer right and follow a path uphill for 200 yards before entering Parsonage Wood. Follow the path ahead through the woodland for 600 yards to a junction at the end of the woodland, turn left and, in 20 yards, turn left and follow a footpath that drops downhill to join a road on the edge of Castle Combe. Turn left and walk through the village to reach a bridge that crosses the By Brook. In another 300 yards, just outside of the village, veer right onto a footpath that climbs uphill through Becker's Wood.

❸ In ¼ mile, on the edge of the woodland, cross a stile and turn left along a lane. In 25 yards, cross a stile on the right, turn left and follow a path that runs parallel to the road along to an information board. Follow the path beyond this information board through woodland to reach a stile and hilltop field. Follow the path ahead across the hilltop for 300 yards

18

to a marker post, before bearing right and dropping downhill to reach a stone slab stile and a footbridge over a river. Beyond this bridge, cross a stile and walk ahead along the right edge of a field. At the end of this field, veer right into some woodland and follow a path through the tree cover to an open field. Walk ahead to the left corner of this field and an information board, before following a back lane to the A420. Turn right, then first left, back to the White Hart.

PLACES OF INTEREST NEARBY

The historic market town of **Corsham** lies just 4 miles from Ford. The town's prosperity was based upon the woollen trade and quarrying. The High Street has a definite Cotswold feel, and visitors will enjoy its selection

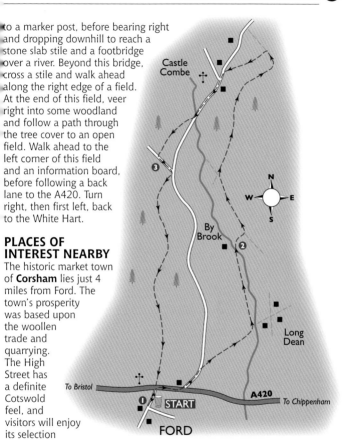

of independent shops. There is also **Corsham Court** (www.corsham-court.co.uk), a privately owned historic house with a significant art collection and attractive gardens.

View of Box

6 Box Hill

4 miles (6.4 km)

WALK HIGHLIGHTS

From Roman times until 1969, golden limestone was extracted from deep beneath Box Hill; stone that was to form the building blocks of many of the properties in the region. The By Brook has become a prized trout fishery and supports a rich array of birdlife, including Dippers and Grey Wagtail, Kingfisher and Heron. The walk passes through the village of Box, where Peter Gabriel's Real World Studio will catch the eye, before climbing steeply uphill to Hazelbury Common and Manor. The common has an enviable reputation for its butterfly population that includes the Gatekeeper and the Essex Skipper, while parts of the Manor date from the 14th century.

THE PUB

The Quarryman's Arms www.quarrymans-arms.co.uk
☎ 01225 743569 **SN13 8HN**

HOW TO GET THERE AND PARKING: Box lies on the A4 between Bath and Chippenham. On the Chippenham side of the village, opposite the Box Surgery, turn right into Bargates. Follow this estate road up to its junction with Box Hill, turn left and drive uphill for 600 yards to a junction by a small green. Turn left along to Box Common, and continue for 100 yards to find the Quarryman's Arms. There is a small car park at the pub. You may want to park on the roadside in the vicinity of Box Common whilst walking. **Postcode** SN13 8HN

MAP: OS Explorer 156 Chippenham & Bradford-on-Avon. **Grid ref** GR 835693.

THE WALK

Walk towards the A4 with The Quarryman's Arms on the left, before reaching a junction immediately past a property called Hillcrest. Bear left down Barnetts Hill and, in 75 yards, at a crossroads, follow Hedgesparrow Lane opposite down to the A4. Cross this main road and follow a lane opposite for ¼ mile down to Drewett's Mill and the By Brook. Having crossed the river, turn left in 20 yards and follow a lane for 50 yards before

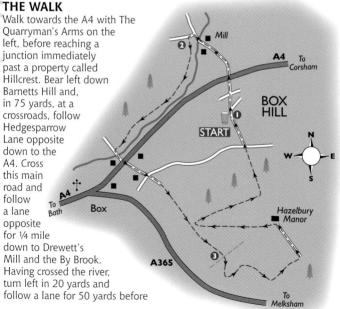

passing through a handgate on the left. Follow the left edge of the field ahead to another handgate and a field above the By Brook.

2 Bear right and walk the length of this riverside meadow to a gate at the far end of the field. Walk the whole length of the next field, the By Brook on the left, to a gate at the far end of the field by the river. Beyond this gate, follow a path to the right that winds its way around to a road by the Real World Studios. Turn left and follow what is Mill Lane for 300 yards up to the A4. Cross over and follow Bulls Lane for 150 yards up to a junction, before following Hazelbury Hill opposite. In 250 yards, where the road ends by Hazelbury Cottage, continue uphill along a footpath for 200 yards to a junction of paths. Follow the bridleway opposite which drops downhill to reach a crossroads of paths in 300 yards.

3 Follow the path opposite that climbs uphill to emerge onto Hazelbury Common in ¼ mile. Turn left and walk up the left edge of the common to reach the entrance gates to a driveway leading to Hazelbury Manor. Turn left and walk the length of the driveway to the manor, before turning left along to a gate and enclosed track that runs across the middle of an open field. On the far side of the field, cross a stile, join an enclosed path and turn right to walk across the hilltop, views to the left across the By Brook valley towards Colerne. At a junction in 350 yards, turn left into an area of woodland and keep on the path as it bears right along the edge of this woodland. In 350 yards, the woodland path reaches a road junction at the top of Box Hill. Follow the road opposite along to Box Hill Common and your vehicle.

PLACES OF INTEREST NEARBY

Dick Willows, a traditional cider maker whose site is also home to boutiques, galleries, a farm shop and a café, lies 2 miles along the A4 from Box in the direction of Bath. Visit www.bath.co.uk and search for 'Dick Willows' for further information.

Mill at Avoncliff

7 Freshford and Dundas Wharf

7 miles (11.3 km)

WALK HIGHLIGHTS

Dundas Aqueduct is named after Charles Dundas, the first Chairman of the Kennet and Avon Canal Company. Its three arches are 150 yards long, built of Bath stone with a central arch that spans 64 feet. Just over three miles down the Kennet and Avon Canal is the slightly smaller but equally impressive Avoncliff Aqueduct. Away from the canal, this walk explores a section of the Avon Valley that takes in the villages of Limpley Stoke, Freshford and Avoncliff.

THE PUB

The Inn at Freshford www.theinnatfreshford.com
☎ 01225 722250 **BA2 7WG**

THE WALK

Drop down the steps at the Bath end of the layby to emerge onto Dundas Wharf. Follow the towpath ahead, passing the entrance to

HOW TO GET THERE AND PARKING: Follow the A36 south from Bath for 5 miles to Monkton Combe before parking in a layby on the left-hand side of the road shortly before a garage and some traffic lights that mark the junction with the B3108 road leading to Bradford on Avon. **NOTE:** This is a walk to a pub so the pub's postcode and the start postcode differ. **Postcode** BA2 7HY

MAP: OS Explorers 142, 155 and 156 all overlap on this walk. **Grid ref** GR 784626.

the Somerset Coal Canal before crossing Dundas Aqueduct. Continue following the towpath, it shortly bears right, and continue for 1 mile to the next canal bridge that carries the B3108 over the Kennet and Avon Canal. Immediately before this bridge, cross a stile on the right and join the B3108.

2 Follow this road to the right, passing over the River Avon and passing under a railway bridge, before turning left into Limpley Stoke village. In 500 yards, at the bottom of Crowe Hill, turn left down a track and under a railway bridge before passing through a gateway to enter a field by the River Avon. Turn right and follow a path across a riverside meadow, passing a belt of trees, to reach a second field. Cross this field, passing to the right of a sewage treatment works, before joining a track. Follow this track around to Freshford Station, cross the footbridge to the opposite platform and leave the station to join Station Road. Follow Station Road for 250 yards to its junction with 'The Hill'.

3 Turn left and walk down to The Inn at Freshford. Continue along the road, cross the River Frome and pass through a handgate on the left. Cross the field ahead to a handgate in its far right corner. Follow a concrete path that runs alongside the River Avon to another gate, before crossing a riverside meadow to reach a kissing gate at the far end of the field. Follow an enclosed path to another gate, before following the lane ahead past Ancliff Square to reach Avoncliff Aqueduct. Climb some steps up to the canal, turn left and cross the aqueduct and follow the Kennet and Avon Canal for 3¼ miles back to Dundas Wharf. Retrace your steps back up to the layby.

PLACES OF INTEREST NEARBY

Claverton Pumping Station (www.claverton. org.uk), that pumps water from the River Avon into the Kennet and Avon Canal, lies just 2 miles north of the start of this walk. The pump started work in 1813 and uses the power of the Avon to lift water 48 feet into the canal. The **American Museum** (www. americanmuseum. org), the only museum of American decorative and folk art outside of the United States, is located in Claverton just 2 miles from the Dundas Aqueduct.

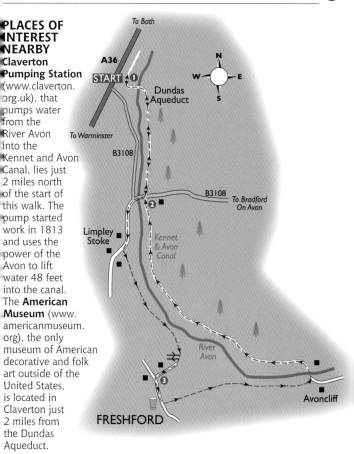

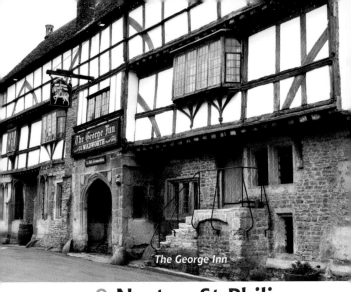

The George Inn

8 Norton St Philip

4½ miles (7.2 km)

WALK HIGHLIGHTS

Maxwell Fraser's *Companion into Somerset* writes of a country lane
leading to Norton St Philip. He talks of a settlement that is 'too lovely
to be overlooked or neglected'. What caught Fraser's eye were the
enchanting black and white inn – reputed to be the oldest in England
– and a fine old church. Behind that enchanting inn – the George
– lies a large open green known as the Mead that runs down to the
parish church. It is the tower that dominates, seventy feet of lovingly
crafted stone that allegedly brought Samuel Pepys to this corner of
Somerset.

THE PUB

The George Inn www.georgeinnnsp.co.uk/home
☎ 01373 834224 **BA2 7LH**

HOW TO GET THERE AND PARKING: Norton St Philip lies on the B3110 Woolverton road, 5 miles south of Bath. In the centre of the village, alongside the George Inn, turn right onto the A366 road for Radstock. In 250 yards, turn left into Vicarage Lane and park alongside the village church. **Postcode** BA2 7LH

MAP: OS Explorer 142 Shepton Mallet & Mendip Hills East. **Grid Ref** 772557.

THE WALK

From Vicarage Lane, return to the A366, turn left and take the first right into Ringwell Lane. Follow Ringwell Lane for 250 yards around to a crossroads. Turn left into Wellow Lane, and follow this quiet road for just over 1 mile to a ford and footbridge on the left, ignoring a track on the left along the way. Cross the Norton Brook at this point, and follow the byway ahead for 1 mile up to Upper Baggridge Farm, ignoring a right turn to Lower Baggridge Farm along the way. Walk through the farmyard to reach a lane. Follow the lane ahead for ½ mile – ignoring the right turn – for 350 yards to a road junction with a lane going off on the right.

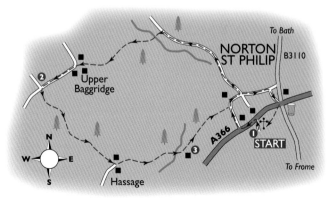

2 At this point, pass through a handgate on the left and drop downhill to a gateway in the bottom field boundary. Drop downhill in the next field and, on reaching the bottom field boundary, turn left. In 20 yards, bear right into the adjoining field and follow its left edge down to its lower left-hand corner, join a track and continue for 350 yards up to a farming hamlet called Hassage. Where the drive bears right at the entrance to Hassage House, keep ahead along an unmetalled track and continue for 400 yards until an old barn appears on the right, ignoring one left turn along the way. Beyond the old barn, follow the track into a field and continue ahead to a point where the wall on the left ends. At this point, bear right and head downhill towards the clearly visible Mount Pleasant Farm. Follow the well defined path downhill to a footbridge that crosses a river.

3 Beyond this bridge, walk ahead to a stile over a fence, keep ahead for a few paces before turning left along an enclosed bridleway. In 200 yards, beyond a gateway, follow an enclosed track for 600 yards back to Ringwell Lane in Norton. Turn left, and follow this lane around to a crossroads in 100 yards. Follow the road opposite – Chevers Lane – and continue uphill for 150 yards before turning right into North Street. Follow this back road through to the A366, and turn left up to the George Inn. Just before the pub follow a path down an alleyway to the Mead, beyond which is the church.

PLACES OF INTEREST NEARBY
Farleigh Hungerford Castle (www.english-heritage.org.uk/visit/places/farleigh-hungerford-castle) lies less than 3 miles east of Norton St Philip on the A366 road to Trowbridge. This fortified mansion was occupied for 300 years by the remarkable Hungerford family and today their intriguing, yet sometimes gruesome stories are told through graphic interpretation panels and a free audio tour.

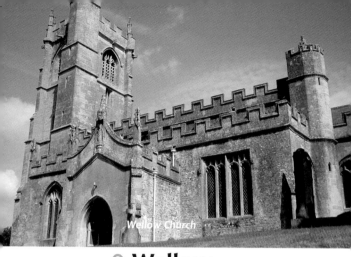

Wellow Church

9 Wellow

5 miles (8 km)

WALK HIGHLIGHTS

Dominating the pretty village of Wellow is St Julian's Church, with its impressive Somerset Perpendicular tower. A steep climb out of Wellow brings the walk into the neighbouring valley and Combe Hay.

THE PUB

The Fox & Badger www.thefoxandbadger.com
☎ 01225 832293 **BA2 8QG**

THE WALK

With your back to the pub, turn right along the main street in Wellow and walk along as far as St Julian's church. Immediately past the church, turn left along an access lane and walk up to a gate. Follow the path ahead across two paddocks to reach Twinhoe Lane. Cross to a gate opposite, and follow right edge of the field ahead up to a stile and large field. Walk ahead, dropping downhill into a dip where hedgerows form a corner, before following the line of a hedge uphill to a gate and lane.

29

Guide to Bristol & Bath Pub Walks

HOW TO GET THERE AND PARKING: Leave the B3110 Bath to Woolverton road by the Stag Inn at Hinton Charterhouse and follow an unclassified road signposted Wellow. Drive 2 miles and the **Fox & Badger** lies in the village centre. There is roadside parking. **Postcode** BA2 8QG

MAP: OS Explorer 142 Shepton Mallett & Mendip Hills East and 155 Bristol & Bath. **Grid ref** 740583.

Turn left and walk along the hilltop for 600 yards to crossroads. Turn right – waymarked Bath and Combe Hay – and follow road for 250 yards to a footpath on right in an area of woodland. Follow footpath into a hillside field above Combe Hay, turn left and drop downhill to a marker post above a belt of trees. Drop downhill through trees to a handgate, before crossing the following field to a handgate opposite – there are marker posts. Drop down to a handgate and follow a section of path down to, and across, the Cam Brook. Keep ahead in the next field to a gate and seat, before following a path up to a gate and road in Combe Hay.

2 Turn right, and follow the road as it winds through Combe Hay, bearing left by the church and right in 50 yards to reach the Wheatsheaf Inn. Continue past the Wheatsheaf for 200 yards, before forking left along a cul-de-sac lane leading to Rowley Farm. Continue to property called East Rowley, where the lane becomes a track. Follow this track for 200 yards to a gate with stile on right. Cross stile, and drop down right edge of a field to enter Engine Wood in bottom corner of the field. In a few paces, turn left, and follow a path alongside an early cut of the Somerset Coal Canal. Follow this path downhill through the woodland to reach the canal's sharp 300° turn. Cross a footbridge over a stream and, in 20 yards, follow the path to the right that borders the locks. Follow this path down to a gate, overbridge and lane. Cross this lane to a handgate opposite, and follow enclosed path for 300 yards to a gate and junction.

3 Turn right, and follow track that crosses Cam Brook before climbing steeply uphill through trees to reach a junction with larger track in ¼ mile. Follow this track to the right to the lane in Twinhoe. Turn left

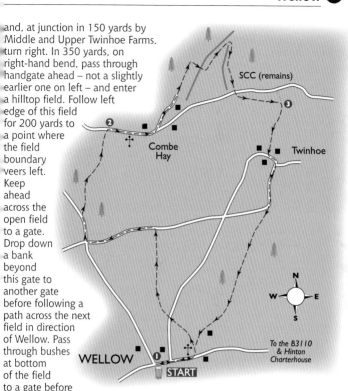

and, at junction in 150 yards by Middle and Upper Twinhoe Farms, turn right. In 350 yards, on right-hand bend, pass through handgate ahead – not a slightly earlier one on left – and enter a hilltop field. Follow left edge of this field for 200 yards to a point where the field boundary veers left. Keep ahead across the open field to a gate. Drop down a bank beyond this gate to another gate before following a path across the next field in direction of Wellow. Pass through bushes at bottom of the field to a gate before following an enclosed path that winds to a gate in 150 yards. Follow left edge of the field ahead to a gate, turn left and walk down the side of the churchyard to Wellow's High Street before turning right back to the Fox & Badger.

PLACES OF INTEREST NEARBY

Radstock Museum (www.radstockmuseum.co.uk).

10 Swineford

6 miles (9.7 km)

WALK HIGHLIGHTS

The tale of Swineford's naming is legendary. Prince Bladud and his pigs were the victims of leprosy. Crossing the shallows in the village, the pigs swam upstream to Bath, rolled around in the mud by the city's springs and were miraculously cured. Bladud founded a city at Bath and dedicated its curative powers to the Celtic goddess Sul, and 900 years later the Romans named the city Aquae Sulis or the 'Waters of Sul'. This is a magnificent walk with views encompassing Salisbury Plain, the Mendip Hills, the Bristol Channel and the Welsh coast.

THE PUB

The Swan www.bathales.com/swan
☎ 0117 932 3101 **BS30 6LN**

THE WALK

1 Facing the pub, follow the A431 to the left before taking the first right, an access road leading to Swineford picnic area. Walk up the left edge

HOW TO GET THERE AND PARKING: Follow the A431 from Bath out through Kelston to Swineford where the Swan is on the right-hand side. There is roadside parking opposite the pub. **Postcode** BS30 6LN

MAP: OS Explorer 155 Bristol & Bath. **Grid ref** 692691.

of the picnic area to a handgate on the left. Enter a field, turn right and follow the edge of the field up to a gate. Continue uphill on an enclosed path to join a road in Upton Cheyney in 350 yards. Turn right, pass the Upton Inn and continue for 200 yards before turning right into Lansdown Lane, a cul-de-sac, ignoring the earlier North Stoke Lane. Follow Lansdown Lane for just over one mile until it ends at a gate just past a cottage. Beyond this gate, follow what becomes a track uphill for ¼ mile to a gate on the hilltop just by a row of conifer trees.

Beyond this gate, follow the track ahead across Lansdown Golf Course for 350 yards to a point where the woodland on the left ends by a

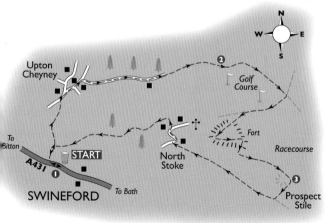

Cotswold Way marker post. Turn right and follow a track for ¼ mile to a gate on the edge of the golf course. Continue downhill, enjoying the stunning view, to a junction in 200 yards. Veer left off the track to a gate and follow a flat grassy path ahead, keeping to the left of a field, to reach a marker post in 200 yards. Turn left and walk uphill to a gate and Little Down Hillfort. Walk across the hillfort's enclosure to a gap opposite before turning right to walk down to the bottom right corner of a field. Turn left in the corner and walk along to a gate and Bath Racecourse. Walk ahead to the corner of the field and a topograph at a point known as 'Prospect Stile' – now replaced by a gate.

3 Pass through the gate and follow a path to the left downhill to another gate and Shiner's Wood. Walk down the left edge of this recently planted woodland to the next gate and a track. Follow this track to the right across the hilltop for one mile to a road junction in North Stoke. Turn right and, in 100 yards, by the entrance to Chestnut Barn, follow a byway on the left. Keep on this byway, it shortly bears left by the Coach House. Continue on this byway as it bears right in 200 yards and continue downhill for ¼ mile to a gate and hillside field. Walk across two fields, passing through gateways along the way, to return to the picnic area. From here walk towards the A431 and turn left to return to the pub.

PLACES OF INTEREST NEARBY

Continue along the A431 towards Bristol for just one mile and you will come to the **Avon Valley Railway** at Bitton (www.avonvalleyrailway. org). This Midland Railway link between Bristol and Bath was closed in the 1960s but, thanks to the efforts of an enthusiastic group of volunteers, three miles of track have been re-laid and locomotives and carriages restored. The Avon Valley once again echoes to the sound of steam.

View from Saltford Lock

11 Keynsham

7 miles (11.3 km)

WALK HIGHLIGHTS

The Lock Keeper at Keynsham enjoys an enviable location, with a stunning riverside outlook alongside the River Avon. From this 300-year-old inn, this walk follows fieldpaths across to the Bristol and Bath Railway Path. This shared-use footpath and cycleway was constructed on the trackbed of the Midland Railway that used to run from Bristol Temple Meads to Bath Green Park via Mangotsfield. Alongside the Railway Path runs a section of preserved Avon Valley Railway.

THE PUB

The Lock Keeper www.lockkeeperbristol.com
☎ 0117 986 2383 **BS31 2DD**

HOW TO GET THERE AND PARKING: Leave the A4 east of Keynsham to follow the B3116 into Keynsham's town centre. Turn right by the church onto the A4175 that leads to Willsbridge and Bitton. In 600 yards, having crossed the River Avon, turn right into a road leading to Portavon Marina. Bear right on this road to reach the Lock Keeper. There is roadside parking. **Postcode** BS31 2DD

MAP: OS Explorer 155 Bristol & Bath. **Grid Ref** 659689.

THE WALK

1 Walk towards The Lock Keeper before following a footpath on the left signposted to Swineford. Follow this path, it initially borders a marina, until it joins a metalled access road in 250 yards. Follow this access road across to a whitewashed property called Avondale House. Where the road bears left into this property, keep ahead across to a field to a gateway opposite. Follow the left edges of the next two fields to a gate, walk along an enclosed section of footpath that passes the entrance to Meadow Wood on the left, and enter the following field. Head across to a gate in the far left corner of this field, passing a stone outbuilding along the way. Follow the left edge of the next field to a gate, before climbing the steps ahead up to the Railway Path.

2 Follow this path to the right for just under two miles to Saltford. Keep ahead on the Railway Path for 100 yards to a bridge that spans the River Avon. Immediately before this bridge, bear left and follow a path that drops down to a road in Saltford. Follow this road around to the right – it soon borders the River Avon. On reaching a boatyard in ¼ mile, veer right and follow a footpath that borders the Avon before reaching Saltford Lock and the car park of the Jolly Sailor pub. Walk through the car park to a road and turn right, walking along to the entrance to Saltford Sewage Treatment Works.

3 Pass through a gateway to the right at this point and follow a grassy path ahead to a gate before following the left edge of a field to the next gate. Beyond this gate, turn right and follow a path down to the River Avon. Turn left and follow a riverside path downstream for one mile to a bridge that carries the Railway Path over the Avon. Immediately past

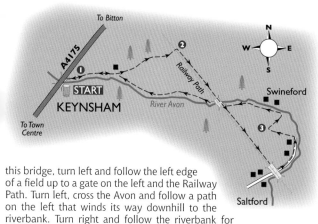

this bridge, turn left and follow the left edge
of a field up to a gate on the left and the Railway
Path. Turn left, cross the Avon and follow a path
on the left that winds its way downhill to the
riverbank. Turn right and follow the riverbank for
1¼ miles back to the access road leading to Avondale House. Retrace
your steps to the left along this road, bearing left onto a footpath 200
yards that brings the walk back past the marina to The Lock Keeper.

PLACES OF INTEREST NEARBY

The Avon Valley Railway (www.avonvalleyrailway.org) has its
headquarters at Bitton Station, less than 2 miles from the Lock Keeper.
Opened in 1869 by the Midland Railway as a through-route between
Birmingham and the South Coast, the line was later linked to the iconic
Somerset & Dorset Railway.

12 Compton Dando

5 miles (8 km)

WALK HIGHLIGHTS

Dominating Compton Dando is the Gothic style St Mary's Church, originally built in the 14th century. A pleasant pastoral landscape lies between Compton Dando and neighbouring Burnett, with a highlight being a well-preserved section of the Wansdyke – a division between British Celtic kingdoms, or boundary with the Saxons. The walk also takes in the River Chew, a noted trout fishery.

THE PUB

The Compton Inn www.thecomptoninn.co.uk
☎ 01761 490321 **BS39 4JZ**

THE WALK

1 With your back to the Compton Inn, follow the road in Compton Dando to the right. In 75 yards, turn right by a war memorial onto Bathford Hill to reach 'The Green' and a bridleway on the right in 350 yards. Keep ahead on the road for another 200 yards to a junction where a road

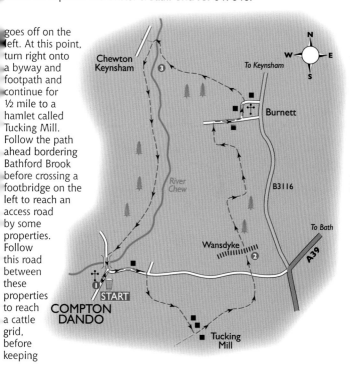

HOW TO GET THERE AND PARKING: An unclassified road at the junction of the A39 and the B3116, 3 miles southwest of Bath, leads to Compton Dando. Alternatively, an unclassified road leaves the B3116 south of Keynsham to reach the village. The Compton Inn is opposite the church in the centre of Compton Dando. There is roadside parking. **Postcode** BS39 4JZ

MAP: OS Explorer 155 Bristol & Bath. **Grid ref** 647646.

goes off on the left. At this point, turn right onto a byway and footpath and continue for ½ mile to a hamlet called Tucking Mill. Follow the path ahead bordering Bathford Brook before crossing a footbridge on the left to reach an access road by some properties. Follow this road between these properties to reach a cattle grid, before keeping ahead for ¼ mile to reach a junction just beyond another cattle grid. Pass through the handgate opposite and walk across the field ahead to reach a handgate opposite by a section of the Wansdyke – if the field is muddy, walk around the right edge of the field to reach the same point.

2 Walk across the next field, bearing right to reach the closest patch of woodland ahead. Follow the edge of this woodland, the woodland on the right. Where the woodland ends, bear half right uphill to reach a handgate in the top field boundary. Beyond this gateway, follow a footpath that winds its way across country for ½ mile to reach the road on the edge of Burnett. Turn right, pass Manor Farm before taking the first left to shortly pass St Michael's church on the right. In 100 yards, where the road bears right, follow a track that heads uphill alongside War Cottage to reach a stile. Turn left and follow a path down to a pair of gates in the corner of the field. Continue along an enclosed grassy path across the hilltop to reach a small copse. Enter an open field and walk diagonally across the middle of this field to reach a gate in its opposite corner. Walk ahead uphill, an area of woodland on the left. At the top corner of this woodland, walk across the middle of a large arable field to a gate in its far left corner alongside the River Chew.

3 Beyond this gate, follow the left edge of the next field, the Chew on the left, to reach a gate and track in ¼ mile. Turn left, cross the River Chew and turn left into a riverside field to follow the Two Rivers Way. At the far side of a second field, veer right away from the river, climbing uphill to a gate. Drop downhill in the next field to a gate before following a well defined path through an area of woodland for 250 yards to a gate. Follow the left edges of the next two fields before continuing along a grassy path to a gate and the road on the edge of Compton Dando. Turn left, cross the Chew and continue along the road back to the Compton Inn.

PLACES OF INTEREST NEARBY

The much acclaimed **Newton Farm Shop and Café** (www. newtonfarmfoods.co.uk) is located in Newton St Loe, just a few miles from Compton Dando on the road back to Bath. Owned and run by a third-generation farming family, local meats are their speciality.

Clevedon Pier

13 Clevedon

6 miles (9.6 km)

WALK HIGHLIGHTS

This delightful walk includes a section of the coastal path bordering the Bristol Channel that runs between Portishead and Clevedon, a path that provides extensive views towards the South Wales coast and the Welsh hills. Before reaching the sea, however, a low range of hills is followed north-eastwards out of Clevedon, taking in both Castle Hill with its 17th-century folly and Walton Down with its ancient field systems and enclosures.

THE PUB

The Moon & Sixpence www.moonandsixpenceclevedon.co.uk
☎ 01275 872443 **BS21 7QU**

THE WALK

With your back to the pub, follow Marine Parade to the right past the pier and on for 200 yards to its junction with Marine Hill by a Catholic church. At this point, fork left onto a tarmac coastal path and continue

41

Guide to Bristol & Bath Pub Walks

HOW TO GET THERE AND PARKING: Leave the M5 at Junction 20 and follow the signs for Clevedon's seafront. The Moon & Sixpence lie on the seafront as you approach the pier. There is roadside parking in front of the pub. **Postcode** BS21 7QU

MAP: OS Explorer 154 Bristol West & Portishead. **Grid Ref** 402719

for ¾ mile to a crossroads of paths. At this point, steps on the right lead up to a road, and the path on the left drops down to Layde Bay. Ignoring these turnings, keep ahead on the main coast path that climbs above Layde Bay. In 400 yards, at the next junction by the remains of an old stile, turn right and climb steeply uphill away from the sea. In 300 yards at the top of the climb, keep on the path as it bears left, all the while bordering the local golf course. Continue along this hilltop path for 250 yards to a stile and a junction.

2 Turn right, and follow a path down to a gate and a drive by the golf course clubhouse. Continue along this access road, passing Keeper Cottage and Cobblestone Cottage, to a junction and turn left. Follow what becomes an unmetalled road along to a handgate, ignoring side turns, and continue along the path as it crosses the golf greens. Beyond these greens, follow the path ahead as it drops downhill through an area of woodland, keeping right on the main path at an early fork. In 350 yards, beyond a handgate, cross another golf green and rejoin the enclosed footpath opposite. Continue downhill through another area of woodland until the path reaches Walton in Gordano church in 200 yards. Follow the path to the left of the church to a lane, and turn right past Church Farm down to the B3124.

3 Turn left and, in 100 yards, just past the last property on the left in Walton in Gordano, cross a stile on the left and enter a field that has been divided up into paddocks. Walk uphill to a stile at the entrance to some woodland 150 yards ahead, crossing one other stile along the way. Beyond this stile, follow the path uphill through the tree cover towards Walton Common. In 200 yards, at a junction, turn right and follow a path that climbs more gently uphill onto the open hilltop. Follow the path across the hilltop ahead, keeping left at a fork along the way

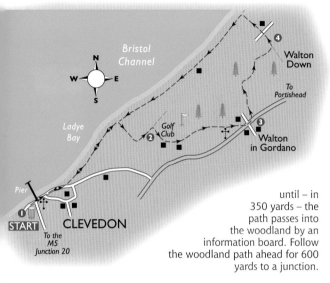

until – in
350 yards – the
path passes into
the woodland by an
information board. Follow
the woodland path ahead for 600
yards to a junction.

Turn left at this T-junction, drop down out of the tree cover and follow a farm road ahead up to some properties on the coast road running between Clevedon and Portishead. Cross this road, and follow the enclosed path opposite that drops down to a stile and a field above the sea. Head down to the bottom left-corner of this field, cross a stile beyond some bushes and join the coast path. Turn left, and follow this path for 2 miles back to Ladye Bay. Beyond this point, retrace your steps along the coast path back to Marine Parade, where a right turn brings you back to Clevedon Pier.

PLACES OF INTEREST NEARBY

Clevedon Court (www.nationaltrust.org.uk/clevedon-court) and **Tyntesfield** (www.nationaltrust.org.uk/tyntesfield) are two National Trust properties a mile-or-two outside of Clevedon.

On Crook Peak

14 Cross and Crook Peak

4 miles (6.4 km)

WALK HIGHLIGHTS

Although a mere 627 ft in height, Crook Peak has a distinctive mountain shape and was a landmark for centuries for sailors navigating the Bristol Channel. There is a 360° panoramic view from the summit that encompasses much of the South Wales coast, vast swathes of the Somerset Levels and Glastonbury's famous Tor.

THE PUB

The New Inn www.newinncross.co.uk
☎ 01934 732455 **BS26 2EE**

❶ THE WALK

Facing the New Inn, follow the Old Coach Road to the left, walking away

44

HOW TO GET THERE AND PARKING: Leave the A38 at its junction with the A371 west of Axbridge and follow an unclassified road into the village of Cross. Almost immediately, the New Inn is on the right-hand side. There is roadside parking on Old Coach Road, in the vicinity of the pub. **Postcode** BS26 2EE

MAP: OS Explorer 153 Weston-super-Mare & Bleadon Hill. **Grid Ref** 418548

from the A38. In 600 yards, take the left turn signposted to Weare and Highbridge. In 250 yards, having crossed the Cheddar Yeo, pass through a gateway on the right and follow a footpath that borders the river. In one mile, having walked across five fields, cross a stile by a gate and join a track. Turn right, cross a bridge and walk up to a gate and lane. Turn right and follow this lane – Rackley Lane – up to its junction with Webbington Road.

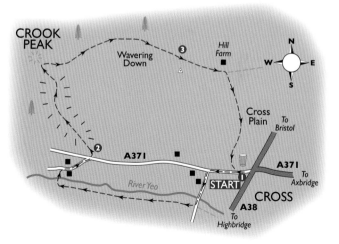

2 Follow a footpath opposite around to a gate and a junction. Ignoring the path ahead, follow the path on the left up through scrubland onto the open ground below Crook Peak. Follow the ridge ahead uphill for ¾ mile to the rocky summit of Crook Peak. From the summit, bear left downhill towards the M5 motorway to the foot of the rocky outcrop. Turn right and follow a path below Crook Peak, walking away from the M5 motorway, before following the course of a drystone wall across Wavering Down to reach a trig point in 1¼ miles.

3 Beyond the trig point, drop downhill to reach Hill Farm on the left and a National Trust 'Cross Plain' sign. At this point, turn right and follow a well-defined ridge (Cross Plain) in a southerly direction. In ¾ mile, where the ridge seemingly ends and drops very steeply downhill, follow a path that veers left making for the A38 and white and pink-washed properties in Cross. In 150 yards, follow a path to the left down to a junction, turn right along to a handgate and follow a path down to the road in Cross. Turn left back to the New Inn.

PLACES OF INTEREST NEARBY

King John's Hunting Lodge (www.nationaltrust.org.uk/king-johns-hunting-lodge) in nearby Axbridge is an early Tudor timber-framed wool merchant's house (circa 1500). Today, it is run as a local history museum by Axbridge and District Museum Trust.

Cheddar Gorge

15 **Cheddar**

4 miles (6.4 km)

WALK HIGHLIGHTS

This is a truly spectacular walk. Cheddar Gorge was carved out of the limestone by rivers that now pass deep underground, leaving vertical cliffs of up to 450 ft in height. Features such as Black Rock Gate and the Horseshoe Bend, the Pinnacles and Lion Rock, convey the drama of this corner of Somerset. From the commercial razzmatazz that is Cheddar village, this walk climbs up the western side of the gorge through the National Trust's 'Cheddar Cliffs' property. The climb is severe, but you will be rewarded with an incredible view.

THE PUB

The Riverside Inn www.riversidecheddar.co.uk
☎ 01934 742452 **BS27 3PX**

Guide to Bristol & Bath Pub Walks

HOW TO GET THERE AND PARKING: Leave the A371 Axbridge to Wells road in Cheddar village and follow the B3135 towards the gorge. In 600 yards, the Riverside Inn is on the right-hand side of the road. Immediately before the Riverside Inn is a public car park (fee payable, but refunded if using the inn). **Postcode** BS27 3PX

MAP: OS Explorer 141 Cheddar Gorge & Mendip Hills West. **Grid Ref** 462536

THE WALK

① Facing the Riverside Inn, follow the B3135 to the left up towards Cheddar Gorge. In ¼ mile, opposite Café Gorge on the right, follow a footpath on the left between gateposts bearing a 'Gorge Walk' logo. The gateposts mark the entrance to an access drive and carry a 'no parking' warning. In 20 yards, climb some steps on the right to follow the Gorge Walk permissive path steeply uphill. At the top of the climb where the path emerges onto open ground, pass through a gateway and follow the path ahead across to a stone wall.

② Follow this path for one mile to a point where it drops down a steep flight of steps, signposted the 'Gorge Walk' all the while. At the bottom of these steps, rather than following the Gorge Walk to the right down to the main road, cross the wall ahead using a series of steps and follow a footpath ahead. Beyond a gate, continue along the path as it runs through woodland and passes through a clearing before dropping downhill into the Black Rock Reserve. Pass through a gateway on the right and walk along to the B3135.

③ Cross the B3135 and follow a steep rocky footpath opposite signposted to Draycott. In 250 yards, pass through a gateway on the hilltop and continue for 75 yards to a marker post and fork. Follow the right-hand path for 250 yards to another gate before continuing ahead to open ground high above Cheddar Gorge with fine views. Follow the path

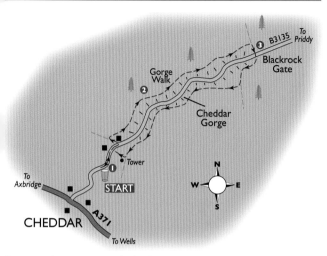

for one mile to a gate and a lookout tower. Immediately past this gate, turn right and descend a flight of steps known as Jacob's Ladder. At the bottom of these steps, pass through a turnstile to join the B3135 road in Cheddar. Turn left back to Riverside Inn.

PLACES OF INTEREST NEARBY

No visit to Cheddar is complete without a visit to the **Cheddar Caves** (www.cheddargorge.co.uk). Gough's Cave is the most beautiful stalactite cavern in Britain, and was also the place where the country's oldest skeleton was found. Cox's Cave, with its magical and mysterious depths, offers the chance to discover the rise of our ancestors.

The **Cheddar Gorge Cheese Company** (www.cheddaronline.co.uk) is the only business that now produces cheese in Cheddar. There is a visitors' centre where you can watch Cheddar cheese being made, matured and packaged. A 20-minute long film summarises the daily manufacturing process should you prefer not to stay for the seven-hour real-time experience!

View of Blagdon Lake

16 Blagdon

8 miles (12.9 km)

WALK HIGHLIGHTS

Blagdon nestles on the north-facing slopes of the Mendip Hills, overlooking the Chew Valley. On the hilltops lie ancient lead workings dating from 49AD. The views are unsurprisingly impressive.

THE PUB

The New Inn www.newinnblagdon.co.uk
☎ 01761 462475 **BS40 7SB**
NB: Children are only allowed in the garden at the New Inn.

THE WALK

1 Walk back up to A368, and follow road opposite – Score Lane. In 250 yards, where this lane ends at a stile, continue ahead along a short section of enclosed footpath to second stile. Keep ahead for 20 yards to marker post where two paths fork. Keep left, and climb up out of woodland into corner of a hillside field. Follow left edge of this field steeply uphill to its top left-hand corner, before following left edge of

50

HOW TO GET THERE AND PARKING: Leave the A368 Weston-super-Mare to Bath road on the eastern edge of Blagdon and turn into Church Street by the village school. In 250 yards, the New Inn is on the right-hand side. Just before the pub, turn left by a small green and park in a cul-de-sac leading up to the church. **Postcode** BS40 7SB

MAP: OS Explorer 141 Cheddar Gorge & Mendip Hills West. **Grid Ref** 505590

the field to a gate and farm track. Follow this track to a gate and lane, just beyond Leaze Farm. Cross lane, and follow green lane opposite. In 150 yards, keep on lane as it bears left to continue across the Mendip hilltops. In ½ mile, pass through a handgate and continue following the path across left-edge of an open field to a handgate and lane. Turn right along this lane – Ubley Drove – and continue for ¾ mile to its junction with B3134.

Cross to gate opposite, and follow right edges of the next two fields to a stile and Nether Wood. Follow path ahead, ignoring all side turns, for

300 yards to a stepped path on right in Charterhouse Mineries site. Turn right, and follow path that runs between two former washing pools to reach stile. Follow footpath ahead up to another stile and road. Turn right along this road for 200 yards, before turning left along a cul-de-sac. Follow this lane for ½ mile to a pair of aerial masts. Continue ahead along the track that passes to the left of these masts for ½ mile to a gateway and open ground of Black Down. Follow right-hand of two paths ahead that climbs uphill to the trig point on Beacon Batch, 600 yards distant.

3 On reaching the trig point, turn right and follow a path down the hillside, heading in a northerly direction. In 600 yards, at bottom of hillside, ignore all side turns at a junction and continue on down a track to join B3134 alongside Ellick House. Turn right, cross cattle grid and take first left, a driveway leading to Lower Ellick Farm. Just before the farmhouse, pass through a gateway on right and follow the line of a fence on left up to a gateway. Beyond this gateway, walk diagonally across the middle of next field to a stile in the opposite hedgerow, almost the field corner. Beyond this stile, turn right to a gate and continue along a byway called Luvers Lane to a junction in 500 yards.

4 Take the second of two roads on right and, in 300 yards, cross stile on left just before the drive leading to Rhodyate Hill Farm. Beyond this stile, follow right edge of a field downhill to a gate in its bottom corner. Continue downhill in second field to a handgate on right, and follow narrow enclosed footpath downhill to a property. Keep on path as it bears left down to a lane. Follow lane downhill to A368, cross to barrier and pavement opposite and follow the pavement to the left. In 100 yards, pass through a gateway on right and follow footpath down through a hillside field to a tarmac path. Follow path to the right for 100 yards to Blagdon church, walk through churchyard and continue along lane back to Church Street.

PLACES OF INTEREST NEARBY

The dam at the western end of **Blagdon Lake** is an excellent spot for birdwatching. Visit www.blagdonlakebirds.com for daily updates on the wildlife that has been seen.

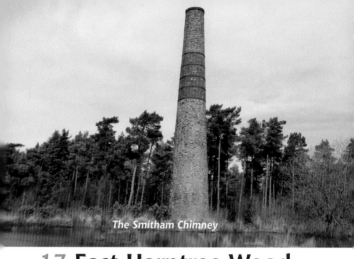
The Smitham Chimney

17 East Harptree Wood
4½ miles (7.2 km)

WALK HIGHLIGHTS
High on the Mendip hilltops lies East Harptree Wood, whose main feature of interest is Smitham Chimney. Lead, silver and calamine were mined and smelted here in the 1850s.

THE PUB
The Castle of Comfort www.thecastleofcomfort.co.uk
☎ 01761 221321 **BS40 6DD**

THE WALK
Leave the car park and turn left along a track leading into woodland. In 400 yards, on a left-hand bend, turn right along waymarked path to Smitham Chimney. Keep on path as far as junction alongside the chimney at the western end of a pond. Turn right and follow a path behind the chimney and downhill to an exit gate from the woodland in 150 yards, ignoring an earlier left turn. Beyond this gate, follow track for 150 yards down past a farm. Turn left beyond a gate along a track to

Guide to Bristol & Bath Pub Walks

HOW TO GET THERE AND PARKING: Leave A39 Bath to Wells road at Green Ore and follow B3135 Cheddar. In 3 miles, at crossroads, turn right onto B3134 Burrington Combe. In ½ mile, with the Castle of Comfort on left, turn right onto a road signposted East Harptree. In 1 mile, turn left into East Harptree Wood car park. Note the pub is a short drive away from the walk. **Postcode** BS40 6DA

MAP: OS Explorer 141 Cheddar Gorge & Mendip Hills West. **Grid ref** 558542

another gate and field. Cross to a gate in middle of end field boundary. In next field, drop downhill to a gate in bottom right corner, bear right to another gate and turn left to drop down left edge of adjoining field to a gate and lane. Turn left along lane and, in 50 yards, pass through a handgate on right before walking across bottom of a field to a gate at entrance to Harptree Combe, 50 yards ahead. Follow path through the combe for ½ mile until it bears right and drops down to a junction. Keep left, and continue following a stream through the combe, passing beneath an aqueduct, to reach a gate and stile in 500 yards.

2 Turn right, and climb a steep bank before walking the length of a narrow field to a stile in the end field boundary. Bear half-right in next field to a stile alongside East Harptree church. Continue along a path to a road before walking down Church Lane to the village store. Follow Whitecross Road ahead for 300 yards to a stile and footpath on right, immediately past an orchard and passing a right turn – Water Street. Cross this stile, and follow the right edges of three fields to a stile and lane alongside some properties. Turn left for just 15 yards, before turning right and following a side lane for 600 yards up to a detached property. Follow the track to the left of this for 150 yards and, where this track ends, pass through a handgate on right and enter a hillside field. Head uphill to a gate in the top field boundary past an isolated tree and, in the following field, head across to a stile in the fence opposite, passing to the right of a telegraph pole. Beyond this stile, walk ahead to a stile in the hedgerow opposite, before crossing the next field to a stile in the opposite field boundary and a track. Follow this track around to the left to junction with another track in just 50 yards, immediately before a lane and property.

Turn right, and follow this stony track uphill for 300 yards to a gate and footpath on right, marked with Monarch's Way marker, ignoring a slightly earlier gateway on right. Follow right edge of this field to a gateway opposite and, in next field, head across to a stile in the opposite field boundary.

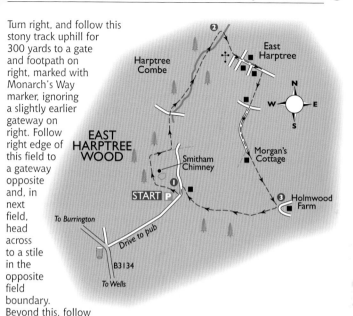

Beyond this, follow left edge of the next field to a gate and track, before continuing along a lane for 250 yards to a road junction just above Pitt Farm. Turn left, and follow lane for 150 yards, before taking a right turn into the Forestry Commission's East Harptree Wood complex. Follow drive ahead, bearing left into the car park.

PLACES OF INTEREST NEARBY

Wells, the smallest city in England, lies just a few miles south (www.wellssomerset.com). Visitors can enjoy the cathedral, the moated Bishop's Palace, and the Wells and Mendip Museum.

Ancient standing stones at Stanton Drew

18 Stanton Drew

5½ miles (8.9 km)

WALK HIGHLIGHTS

Stanton Drew's ancient stones have a degree of anonymity, despite being the third largest stone circle in Britain. The walk includes a stiff climb, but you will be rewarded with fine views across the Chew Valley.

THE PUB

The Druid's Arms www.thedruidsarms.co.uk
☎ 01275 332230 **BS39 4EJ**

THE WALK

1 Leave the car park, turn right past the pub before taking next right signposted 'Village Church'. At junction, follow metalled road ahead that passes a farm before heading to a sewage works. The stone circle is in field on left. 100 yards before the works, pass through a handgate on right and cross a field to a gap in hedgerow opposite. Walk across the next field, bearing slightly right, to a handgate before crossing next field, and small orchard on right, to a gate and lane. Turn left and, in

HOW TO GET THERE AND PARKING: Leave the A37 at Belluton, 7
miles south of Bristol, and follow B3130 Chew Magna. In 1½ miles,
turn left by a whitewashed toll house into Stanton Drew where the
Druid's Arms is on the left-hand side in ½ mile. Turn left past the pub
to park in top section of the car park. **Postcode** BS39 4EJ

MAP: OS Explorer 155 Bristol & Bath. **Grid Ref** 598632

150 yards, pass through a gateway on left and follow left edge of field
ahead to a gate, the Chew on left, before crossing the following field to
a gate by the river. Cross two further fields, heading towards a red brick
property.

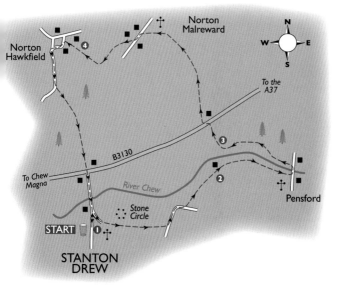

Guide to Bristol & Bath Pub Walks

2 Follow path by property to a gate, then cross next field to a gate. Follow enclosed path to a gate, before crossing the next two fields to reach Pensford Viaduct. Pass under viaduct and cross a footbridge over the Chew before bearing left through the Rising Sun's car park to reach Church Street in Pensford. Turn left and almost immediately left again onto a back road giving access to some properties – signposted footpath. Having passed under Pensford Viaduct, pass through a gateway into Culvery Wood. Follow path ahead that drops downhill to a gate and riverside meadow. Walk across two fields by the Chew and, in a third field, bear right across to a gate where hedgerows form a corner.

3 Beyond this gate, follow hedge on right uphill towards a telegraph pole. At top of the climb, pass through a gate on right and walk ahead to another gate and B3130 by some properties and the drive to Summer House. Turn left and, in 20 yards, turn right onto a byway. In 300 yards, at the top of a climb, pass through a handgate and cross a hilltop field towards Norton Malreward. On the far side of the field, keep left to a gate. Cross a track to a gate opposite before crossing two fields, bearing right, to a gate in the far-right corner of the second field and road. Turn left and, just past the Old Rectory, pass through a gate on right and follow path along edge of a field. In 100 yards, pass through a gate on left and follow path ahead through trees to a gate. Follow path ahead and, in 200 yards, bear right down to a farm in Norton Hawkfield.

4 In the farmyard, bear left between barns to reach a gate and lane. Turn left and then right onto a lane passing Orchard Cottage. Immediately past School Cottage, turn left down a footpath to a lane. Follow lane for 300 yards and, on right-hand bend, climb steps on left to a gate and follow footpath across a hilltop field to a gate where field boundary forms a corner. Follow left edge of the next field to a gate before crossing to a gate in far-right corner of following field. Cross to a gate in right corner of next field before following right edge of the following field to a gate. Drop downhill in the next field to a gate and B3130 by a garage. Turn right to a tollhouse, then left back into Stanton Drew, reaching the pub in ¼ mile.

PLACES OF INTEREST NEARBY
Chew Valley Lake lies less than 3 miles away.

58

View from Prospect Stile

19 **Hinton Blewett**

6 miles (9.7 km)

WALK HIGHLIGHTS

Below Hinton Blewett lie the Litton Lakes, two reservoirs that are a paradise for trout fishing and birdwatching. The walk passes through Chewton Wood before reaching the Hollow Marsh Nature Reserve.

THE PUB

The Ring O' Bells www.ringobellshinton.co.uk
☎ 01761 452239 **BS39 5AN**

THE WALK

From the parking area, cross to the pub and follow the road left around to the church entrance and Upper Road. Follow Upper Road for 250 yards to a junction, keep right and, in 150 yards on bend by a farm, follow the footpath on right. In 25 yards, keep on path as it bears left beyond some farm buildings and continue for 200 yards to a junction. Turn left and follow an enclosed path for 350 yards to a road by Prospect

Guide to Bristol & Bath Pub Walks

HOW TO GET THERE AND PARKING: The B3114 runs from the A39 at Chewton Mendip to the A368 at West Harptree. At Coley, halfway along this road, take the unclassified road to Hinton Blewett. Follow road for 1½ miles into the village. The Ring O' Bells is on the left-hand side. Park by a small green known as 'The Barbury'. **Postcode** BS39 5AN

MAP: OS Explorers 141 Cheddar Gorge & Mendip Hills West and 142 Shepton Mallett & Mendip Hills East. **Grid Ref** 595569.

Stile. Turn left. Ignore a left turn and then right turn to Coley and East Harptree, before taking the next right into Hook Lane.

2 In 200 yards, pass through a gateway on right and cross hilltop field to a stile opposite. Cross the next field to a stile in opposite hedgerow, before crossing the following field to a gate and view of Chew Valley. Drop downhill in next field to a gate in far bottom corner before reaching another gate to the right by Litton's Lower Reservoir. Turn left and follow the path for 350 yards to reach the Upper Reservoir. Continue following the path by the reservoir for ½ mile to a gate and lane. Turn left and, at a junction in ¼ mile, turn right.

3 In 400 yards, turn left along a cul-de-sac lane and continue for ¾ mile until the lane ends at a junction of paths at the entrance to Chewton Wood. Pass through the gateway ahead and follow the main track through wood for ¾ mile to a gate at end of the woodland. Immediately past this gate, pass through a gateway on left and follow right edge of the field ahead to a footbridge in its far corner. Continue ahead along a woodland path to a stile and Hollow Marsh Nature Reserve. Walk along right edge of the reserve to a stile and footbridge in its corner before continuing ahead along an unimproved meadow, still part of the Hollow Marsh Reserve. There are three exits at the end of this meadow; pass through the handgate at the right-hand end of the field, not the gate slightly to its right in the right-hand boundary.

4 Beyond gate, follow right edge of the field ahead uphill. In top corner, turn right then left then right in quick succession to enter a second field.

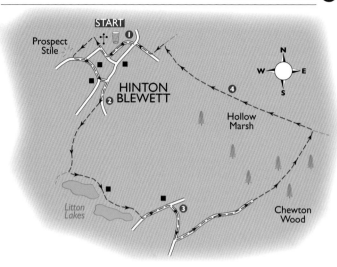

Turn left and follow left edge of the field in direction of Hinton Blewett to a gate in the corner of the field. Drop downhill in the following field, crossing a small stream, before climbing uphill to a gate in the top right corner of the field. Beyond this, follow hedgerow ahead for 20 yards to a point where it forms a corner. Here, turn left and follow line of hedgerow to a gate. Cross next field to a gate opposite, walking in direction of Hinton Blewett church, before crossing the next field to a point where hedgerows form a corner. Follow line of hedge downhill to a gate on left in the bottom corner of the field, before crossing the bottom edge of a final field to a gate and lane by some properties. Turn right and follow the road uphill back to the Ring O' Bells.

PLACES OF INTEREST NEARBY

Follow B3114 into West Harptree, turn right along A368 and in one mile, park in a layby at Herriott's Bridge overlooking the **Chew Valley Reservoir**. This is an excellent spot for birdwatching. (www.cvlbirding.co.uk)

Deer Leap

20 Priddy

6 miles (9.7 km)

WALK HIGHLIGHTS

Priddy is home to a permanent set of sheep hurdles. These commemorate an annual sheep fair, moved to this hilltop in 1348 from Wells on account of the Black Death. The walk follows an exploration of Ebbor Gorge and a scramble up through the gorge itself. This involves a literal 'hands and feet' climb over some rocky boulders, making for a memorable excursion.

THE PUB

The Queen Victoria www.thequeenvicpriddy.co.uk
☎ 01749 676385 **BA5 3BA**

THE WALK

1 Walk back down to the main road through Priddy, turn left and, in 50 yards, follow the side road that runs along the left-hand side of Priddy Green. On the far side of the Green, turn left along a cul-de-sac. At the end of this lane, cross a stile by a bungalow called Trail's End before

62

HOW TO GET THERE AND PARKING: Leave the A39 at Green Ore, 3 miles north of Wells, and follow the B3135 towards Cheddar. In 4 miles, follow a left turn signposted to Priddy. Having passed the village green, turn right along a side road to the Queen Victoria. There is roadside parking or a car park for pub patrons. **Postcode** BA5 3BA

MAP: OS Explorer 141 Cheddar Gorge & Mendip Hills West. **Grid Ref** 528508.

following a footpath directly ahead across four fields, making for a stile in the right-hand corner of the fourth field by a telegraph pole. Cross two further fields to stiles, before walking down the left edge of the next field. At the bottom of this field, cross a stone slab stile on the left-hand side and follow the grassy path ahead across the hillside to a gate and the car-park for Deer Leap.

To the B3135 Cheddar Road

PRIDDY

START ❶

Deer Leap

❷

Higher Pitts Farm

❸

Ebbor Gorge

2 Join a road, turn right and, in 50 yards, cross a stile on the left, turn right and walk across a field to a stile opposite. Cross the next field to a stile alongside a gate, walking in the direction of the distant Tor at Glastonbury. Join a road and turn left, walking downhill for 350 yards before turning left into the Ebbor Gorge parking area. Turn right and walk down through the car park and past a picnic area to a viewpoint on the left overlooking Ebbor Gorge. Continue downhill, descending some steps to reach a gate. 40 yards beyond this gate, turn right at a junction and, in 250 yards, turn left onto a path signposted 'To the Gorge'. Follow this path for 300 yards, scramble up through what is a rocky path, and continue for 100 yards to a junction. Turn right and walk uphill to a junction in 100 yards. At this point, detour to the right where, in 200 yards, you will reach a clifftop viewpoint. Return to the junction and continue following the path ahead up through woodland to reach a second gate in 350 yards and information board.

3 Beyond this gate, follow the left edge of a hilltop field around to a gate and water trough. Do not leave the field at this point – instead, follow the line of a hedgerow to the right down to a stile in a dip. Follow the left edge of the next field as it climbs gently uphill. Immediately beyond this field, cross a stile on the left. Walk down the left edge of the field beyond this stile to join a track called Dursdon Drove. Turn left and follow this drove track for just over ½ mile to reach an enclosed footpath on the right-hand side, ignoring a much earlier bridleway on the right. Follow this footpath around to a stone slab stile. Cross this stile, turn right and follow the right edges of two fields. In the top corner of the second field, turn left and follow the field boundary along to a stile and the road from Deer Leap to Priddy. Turn right to arrive at the Queen Victoria in 600 yards.

PLACES OF INTEREST NEARBY
Wookey Hole Caves (www.wookey.co.uk) lie just 2 miles south of Priddy, boasting 20 attractions including the famous limestone caverns.